LAND USE CONTROL

Land Use Control

Evaluating Economic
and Political Effects

David E. Ervin
James B. Fitch
R. Kenneth Godwin
W. Bruce Shepard
Herbert H. Stoevener

Ballinger Publishing Company ● **Cambridge, Massachusetts**
A Subsidiary of J. B. Lippincott Company

This book is printed on recycled paper.

Material incorporated in this Work was developed with the support of National Science Foundation grant number ESR 74-19412. However, any opinions, findings, conclusions or recommendations expressed herein are those of the authors and do not necessarily reflect the views of the National Science Foundation.

International Standard Book Number: 0-88410-062-6

Library of Congress Catalog Card Number: 76-51214

Printed in the United States of America

Library of Congress Cataloging in Publication Data

Main entry under title:
Land use control.

  Bibliography: p. 167
  1. Land use—Planning—United States. 2. Economic zoning—United States. I. Ervin, David E.
HD205 1977.L36   333.1'0973   76-51214
ISBN 0-88410-062-6

Contents

List of Figures

List of Tables

Foreword

Appreciation for the research reported in this manuscript will be enhanced if one knows something of the genesis of the research, the motivations for the research, and the principal characteristics of the research approach. This foreword is written to that end.

This research grew out of a large multidisciplinary research, educational, and public-service effort at Oregon State University financed by the Rockefeller Foundation. This undertaking involved several departments, schools and colleges on campus and had as its main focus an understanding of the conflicts and issues involved with the people of Oregon simultaneously pursuing two objectives: enhanced environmental quality and increased economic activity.

One of the units involved in this effort was a group of social scientists that came to be known as the Location Decision Unit. This group included an anthropologist, two sociologists, two political scientists and three economists. Others, including a historian, were at various times involved in the work of this unit. The Location Decision Unit was charged with the responsibility for investigating the factors influencing the location of people in Oregon as well as identifying those policies and programs the state might use to influence the size, composition, and location of population and economic activity.

As a consequence of this activity, individual social scientists within the group began to learn a great deal about the disciplines of the others. A number of publications resulted from these investigations that were truly interdisciplinary in nature. That is, concepts were developed and results were generated that would not have been possi-

ble if the representatives of the various social science disciplines had been working independently or in parallel fashion.

As the group continued to explore the policies available to the state and to interact with those in the executive and legislative branch of government it became obvious that much greater knowledge was needed about possible land use policies and controls the state might adopt. On the one hand, there were those who believed that land use controls were the key to managing or preventing the undesirable side effects of economic growth. On the other, it also became apparent that a great many consequences of land use controls were not known.

It was suspected that there might be more to the opposition to land use controls than just the reluctance of the greedy to sacrifice unearned increments in the value of their real property.

In response to this intellectual concern, a group within the Location Decision Unit developed a project and sought funding to permit them to focus on land use policies. The National Science Foundation agreed to finance such a project, and the present book is the result. The project was an ambitious one: it attempted to explore some of the fundamental economic and political implications of land use controls. The length of time NSF allowed for the completion of the project—18 months— meant that it had to be organized carefully and executed with dispatch if it were to be successful.

The project has yielded highly significant results. The authors demonstrate the symmetry that existed between the public and private rights in land use; one cannot significantly enlarge the public sector's rights in land without affecting the exercise of private rights. The exercise of those private rights has, over time, become encrusted and embedded in numerous institutions. Taxation and finance, to mention but two, are based on assumptions with respect to private rights in property. Further, the political ramifications of sweeping changes in land use controls are such that mandatory legislation at either the state or national level seems improbable. Thus the research results suggest the basis for the conservative attitude toward land use controls that often prevails.

But it would be a mistake to conclude that the research results support a particular point of view. They do not. Those who want to promote or draw new land use legislation will find much that is of value. Only by recognition of the realities involved can one expect to make significant progress in this complex field.

As noted earlier, this was a joint undertaking of economists and political scientists. The project leader was Herbert H. Stoevener, resource economist. He took the primary responsibility for preparing Chapters 1 and 2. R. Kenneth Godwin and W. Bruce Shepard, political scientists, wrote Chapter 4. James Fitch, resource economist, is the author of Chapter 7. Mark Erlandson contributed the subject of his master's thesis to the project, and some of his results appear in the latter part of Chapter 3. The heaviest burden of daily coordination and final writing fell on the shoulders of David Ervin, a resource economist, who is the primary author of Chapters 5 and 6.

Emery N. Castle*
Washington, D.C., August 1976

**Formerly Dean of the Graduate
School, Oregon State University,
Currently Vice President and
Senior Fellow, Resources for the
Future.*

Acknowledgments

Financial support for this study was provided by the National Science Foundation, grant No. ESR 74–19412 entitled "Equity Considerations and Compensation Techniques as Related to Increased Public Control of Land Use," by the Oregon Agricultural Experiment Station, the Rockefeller Foundation project No. RF 71079, and the Western Rural Development Center. Any opinions, findings, conclusions, or recommendations expressed in this study remain those of the authors and do not necessarily reflect those of any of the supporting organizations.

The authors have benefited from the help of many individuals. Emery N. Castle was involved in the perception and design of the project. George Carson, Arnold Holden, and John Schefter interacted with the research team at weekly workshops. Daniel Bromely and Norman Wengert reviewed a first draft of the research results and provided helpful suggestions; so did a National Science Foundation panel of reviewers. R. Bruce Rettig, Jean B. Wyckoff and Robert Dawson commented on the chapters concerning economic analysis of different land use techniques.

Much of the typing load fell on Bette Bamford. She was assisted by Audree Berrey, Kristy Sprinker, and Carolyn Johnson. Ronald P. Lovell provided editorial assistance. Clover Redfern typed the final draft.

LAND USE CONTROL

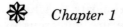

Chapter 1

Introduction

Debates about land use planning currently enjoy an unprecedented popularity. In the United States they cover a broad range of public institutions that might deal with this policy issue. At the national level there is a call for a more explicit statement of a "national land use policy." Presumably, if such a statement were developed, it could lead to a coordinated approach in conjunction with national policies in such areas as taxation, housing, agriculture, energy, transportation, environment, and regional natural-resource developments.

In the absence of an explicit national policy, land use is determined largely by three interdependent forces. First, a myriad of individual decision-makers follow their incentives to maintain or alter existing patterns of land use. The market in land and other real estate is largely a reflection of these forces. As the demands for various types of land use change, prices of land resources suitable for satisfying these demands are affected in accordance with their availability. For example, as the demand for residential land increases in the course of population expansion in an urban area, land prices in and contiguous to the urban area will also increase. Resource owners will take these higher prices into account as they seek to maximize their self-interest in selecting appropriate uses for their land. It has long been argued that under certain conditions the decision-makers' responses to such market signals will lead to the "highest and best use" of land. More will be said later about the violation of some of these conditions, which is likely to lead to less than socially optimal land resource allocations.

The second major set of forces affecting the pattern of land use comprises public policies undertaken primarily to achieve objectives not directly related to land use. There are numerous examples of effects on land use from national policies: several provisions of the federal tax laws relating to the treatment of home mortgage interest, depreciation allowances on commercial real estate, and capital gains in the computation of taxable income, for instance, have affected residential and commercial real estate development in important ways. Nor are these effects restricted to national policies. State governments have had similar effects through their decisions about the location of transportation networks and other state supported facilities, to give only two examples; and at the local level, the location of schools, the extension of public service boundaries, and the manner of their financing are important determinants of land use. These forces, whether they operate through national, state, or local policies, generally affect land use indirectly. They change the market signals to which private decision-makers respond or they modify the incentives for private action in other ways. Because the scope of public policies which impinge upon land use in this manner is so broad, their overall evaluation would be a complex, if not impossible task. A less ambitious, but probably more productive effort would include an analysis of land use effects as part of the general evaluation of these policies.

That such analyses have not been conducted more frequently is perhaps an indication that land use effects have been considered either unimportant or not sufficiently inconsistent with prevailing land use goals to merit public attention. Conditions may now have changed to warrant broader analyses. The building of highways to the suburbs together with federal income tax regulations have fostered a settlement pattern encouraging a large portion of the population to live in single dwelling units, often at considerable distances from their places of work. A study of the relationships between highway construction and taxation policies and settlement patterns may be in order now, as well as an evaluation of various settlement patterns themselves.

The third set of forces affecting land use decisions consists of public policies specifically designed to alter or preserve prevailing land use patterns. Historically these policies have been the prerogatives of local governments in the United States. They are centered on urban land use control, but their use is expanding into rural areas as well. Some of the techniques for implementing land use policy that are traditionally employed by local governments and others that are being considered for more extensive application provide the focus for this study.

Thus, our study deals primarily with those aspects of land use planning that are instruments of explicit land use planning policies.

The general public thinks of land use planning in the terms suggested here.

Our study is directed toward other researchers, members of the planning profession, public officials, and the interested general public. For other economists and political scientists we attempt to provide an evaluation framework for land use policies focusing on economic efficiency, distribution, and political acceptability. There is nothing new in this framework as such. Applying this social science analysis to land use planning is, however, quite new. It is hoped that sketching this analytic approach and applying it to certain land use planning techniques will stimulate others to expand upon the suggested concepts and to apply them more rigorously to the techniques analyzed here or to other aspects of land use planning.

Land use planning, even when viewed as narrowly as proposed here, can have very profound effects on the manner in which land and associated resources are used. Given the important role of land both as a factor of production and as a source of direct satisfaction to the consumer, modifications in the role of land will affect a large number of production and consumption decisions. The complexity of that role necessitates a carefully considered framework within which to evaluate the outcomes.

To derive such an evaluative framework, we started by assuming that some basic dissatisfaction with existing states of affairs causes the public to resort to land use planning. There are two sources of such dissatisfaction. First, there may be a general feeling that the overall outcomes of land use allocation decisions, in terms both of the quantities and types of goods and services produced and of the level of enjoyment yielded by direct use of land resources, were found lacking. It is not difficult to think of examples of land use decisions where the negative effects outweighed the positive. Take, for example, the decision to locate a rock-crushing plant in a quiet residential neighborhood. It is likely that the adverse effects of this decision are greater than the advantage of placing the plant at that particular location. Once such a decision has been made, almost any observer will be able to identify the benefits of avoiding its negative impact. Most will agree that some form of public intervention would have avoided such social wastefulness or inefficiency. It is argued here that this lack of social efficiency is one of the primary reasons for public planning of land use.

There is a danger that our repeated references to *efficiency* in the following chapters will frustrate some of our readers. A caveat may be in order. We argue throughout this volume that the focus on efficiency does *not* imply a preoccupation with counting only *monetary* or *market* benefits and costs. What is said about deviations from the efficiency norm is equally relevant in the case of nonmonetary or nonmarket values as in the case cited above. As a matter of fact, it is largely these values which give rise to public concern in this area. The decision to locate a rock crusher in a residential area may be profitable, and thus efficient, from a narrowly defined market viewpoint which counts only in monetary terms. However, given our broader viewpoint where impacts are taken into account which do not enter a firm's profit calculations, the decision may well be socially inefficient.[1] In this sense we are referring to overall social efficiency. Any later references to *efficiency* are made in this context.

The second part of our evaluative framework concerns the distributive aspects of land use planning decisions. Again, there may be considerable dissatisfaction with the outcome of land use planning decisions in terms of the specific groups which are benefited or disadvantaged by them. At least one of the reasons for preferential property tax treatment of agricultural land was to lessen the tax burden on farmers when rapid urbanization increased agricultural land values and hence ad valorem property taxes.

Efficiency and distributional criteria are not independent of each other. When an especially large burden of the costs of an action are borne by a specific group, that group may call public attention to the action, and subsequent analysis may indicate that the costs imposed on the group render the action inefficient. On the other hand, an apparently "wasteful" action may be tolerated because a disproportionately large share of its benefits accrue to a sector of the population deemed especially worthy of them.

More will be said about the analysis of efficiency and equity in Chapters 2 and 3. Chapter 4 considers the political acceptability of techniques of public land use control. The distribution of the effects of these techniques plays an important role in this political analysis. This concept is not without difficulty: political feasibility is an elusive idea. Nevertheless, the focus on political acceptability helps us to identify some strategies that are more likely to be implemented than others. Moreover, it allows us to predict how specific proposals may be modified in the political arena and how they may be implemented. In the remaining chapters the efficiency, distributional effects, and political acceptability of several land use planning techniques are discussed.

1. The fact that the impact of noise and congestion may eventually become monetarized by depressing residential property values does not alter the nature of the decision.

※ *Chapter 2*

Efficiency Criteria in
Land Use Planning

Many of the arguments in current debates about land use planning are primarily economic. Arguments supporting a zoning change may focus on "highest and best use," while neighborhood residents opposing the change may characterize it as one which would depress the value of their properties. The location of a new highway or school in a certain area may spark controversy because one group perceives it as a means to alleviate congestion or promote desired growth in its neighborhood while another views it as the source of an undesirable increase in housing density and a reduction in the amount of "open space" available. Land requirements for residences, commercial developments, and highways are often most inexpensively met by converting to these urban uses that land which is also best adapted to produce food. Efforts to provide low cost housing and to minimize public expenditures for road construction may conflict with the objective of keeping the most productive cropland in cultivation. Much controversy surrounds the residential settlement pattern per se. Many argue that tighter controls on land use conversion would reduce "sprawl" and hence would result in the attendant benefits of lower costs of public services and lower commuting and transportation costs in general.

These arguments and controversies reflect various aspects of public frustration with the existing state of affairs. Although certain kinds of conflict will exist as long as man's wants exceed his ability to satisfy them, another characteristic is also associated with the examples cited above. In all cases we are dealing with situations where it may be possible through a different set of decisions to effect a superior outcome

5

in the sense that society could be made better off than it is in the existing situation.

Because of our inability objectively to compare one person's satisfaction or pain with that of others, making general comparisons between any two states of affairs and judging unequivocally in which situation society would be better off is still scientifically impossible. There are, however, limited cases in which it is possible for us, at least at the conceptual level, to make some judgments about choosing a preferred outcome. We can say that situation B is preferred over situation A when

1. everyone is better off in B than in A; or
2. at least one person is better off in B and no one is made worse off by moving from A to B; or
3. those who gain by moving from A to B can, out of their gains, compensate those who lose and still be left with a positive net gain.

One of these situations frequently characterizes land use decisions. It may be possible to make such gains in efficiency by changing, through public action, the rules under which land use decisions are made. To put it differently, explicit public policies in land use allocation may lead to increases in social net benefits that would not be obtainable in the absence of such policies. While such benefits may not be achievable for various practical reasons, it may be instructive to think of that set of decision rules which would lead to an optimum allocative outcome. Such an outcome would be optimal in the sense that it would be impossible to change the allocation to bring about further improvements in terms of the criteria set out above.

Economists refer to such an optimal or most efficient allocation of resources as a *Pareto optimum*. It would be advantageous for the purpose of policy analysis if, at least at the conceptual level, the Pareto optimum could be recognized as a unique resource allocative outcome. Other allocations could then be compared to it, and judgments could be made about their deviations from the efficiency norm.

Unfortunately, a Pareto optimum does not represent a unique constellation of outcomes. It is unique only under a particular pattern of distribution of resource endowments or, more broadly, a particular set of rules governing how returns from the use of various resources are to be distributed. It is, however, possible to review the rules themselves to ascertain whether or not they permit a Pareto optimum to be obtained. For our purposes, an important characteristic of these rules is that in each allocation decision they reflect all the beneficial and adverse effects of that decision. In our terminology, an improvement can always be made when account has not been taken of certain benefits or costs; hence there are rules (or systems of property rights) that do not lead to a Pareto optimum. On the other hand, more than one set of rules may also lead to such an optimum. But the rules may differ sharply on how resource returns are to be distributed, thus changing the relative wealth positions of various groups and resulting in different (Pareto-optimal) allocative outcomes. An example to illustrate these points may be helpful

Let us assume that there is an agriculturally used meadow located within a residential area of single family houses. This area itself is situated close to an urban center. The meadow is privately owned and there are no significant public constraints on the owner's alternatives for the use of the meadow.

From the owner's point of view it may be most profitable to convert the meadow to a shopping center, even though this use would have negative spillover effects on the residential neighborhood, effects which the owner would not take into account. The possibility exists at least that the owner would change his development plans were he to take the negative spillovers into consideration. If a consideration of the effects on the residential neighborhood leads to a different outcome, then a decision which does not take these effects into account does not lead to a Pareto-optimal outcome.

As an alternative, let us assume that in this situation the owner's decision-making is not unconstrained and the neighboring property owners hold veto power over his decision to develop the meadow. The likely outcome now is one in which no negative spillovers obtain, perhaps development of the meadow to single family residences. If neighboring property owners gain from the current use of the meadow (e.g., derive "open space benefits" from it), no development will take place at all. Again, it is unlikely that the outcome will be optimal, since the neighboring property owners will fail to take into consideration benefits to the owner likely to result from development of the meadow.

The difficulties and costs of developing the necessary information and administering the solution aside, it is possible to think of a third situation, one in which a public agency specifies the development plan for the meadow taking all relevant effects into account. Specifically, the agency could choose a level of development that would balance at the margin the positive and negative effects of the land use change. It is at least conceptually possible to reach an optimal outcome in this manner.

A fourth situation suggests itself wherein the public agency provides a forum for negotiation between the developer and the neighboring property owners. Perhaps a system such as the "zoning auction" could be used. Again, it is possible to arrive at a Pareto-optimal solution.[1] As in the third case, the outcome would be efficient, although not necessarily identical. In the latter case, the wealth position of one of the affected parties might be greatly different, e.g., the neighboring property owners might be worse off because they had to bid against development. Their changed wealth position would affect the optimal outcome.

We have seen that even at the conceptual level it is not possible to identify just one outcome as optimal. But it may be productive to analyze a decision-making system to see whether it has the necessary characteristics to lead to an efficient solution. If it does not, it will be possible to "make someone better off."

Given the current system of land use decision-making, we argue that possibilities exist for increasing efficiency. Efficiency, in this normative sense, becomes a goal and its pursuit leads to social improvement. But analysis of land use planning decisions in this framework does something else. It allows us to predict the behavior of various parties involved and hence permits us also to analyze changes in the decision-making system undertaken to bring about the achievement of other objectives—for example, to alter the distribution of the effects of land use change. More will be said about the analysis of distributional effects per se in Chapter 3 and their relationship to political acceptability is discussed in Chapter 4. We caution again that all these effects are interrelated, but we want to turn first to some efficiency considerations.

In land use planning, society may gain some efficiencies by concentrating primarily on three areas:

1.   the reduction of certain negative external effects which result from interdependencies among land uses;
2.   the provision of the optimal level of public goods; and
3.   reducing the costs of providing certain public services.

We shall address each of these objectives in turn.[2]

EXTERNAL EFFECTS

The first of the three efficiency goals involves the economic concept of "technological external diseconomies," sometimes called negative *ex-*

---

1. We again exempt from consideration the incidence of information-gathering costs.
2. Clawson provides a similar rationale for social control over private land (1975, pp. 474–476).

ternalities or *external effects*. These exist because of certain technical interdependencies among consumption and/or production processes. Because of these interdependencies, the actions of one individual negatively affect those of another, and the former is given no incentive to account for these "external" effects in his own decision process. These negative external effects provide the conceptual framework within which economists analyze the pollution problem. Unconstrained pursuit of self-interest by one producer leads him to seek the least costly alternative for disposing of his waste; he fails to consider the costs such disposal may impose on others.

It may be that the reduction of these negative external effects has provided a primary rationale for public intervention in land use—particularly for zoning, the most widely used *comprehensive* land use planning tool.[3] How can zoning or other public measures deal with these phenomena? They must be judged by how effectively they increase efficiency through the reduction of these externalities. The costs of the control measure must be lower than the value of the benefits resulting from reducing the externalities.

Zoning is the subject of Chapter 5. Let us indicate briefly here that zoning implies spatial separation of land uses. Many of the harmful effects resulting from physical interdependencies in production and consumption processes can be reduced or eliminated by keeping these processes spatially separated. There must be many circumstances in which such separation could be accomplished at relatively low cost while the benefits derived therefrom are significant. Although land use planners employing zoning have not formally attempted to balance benefits and costs at the margin (as would be required for an economic optimum), early zoning approaches displayed some general characteristics which, at the very least, led in the direction of such an optimum. One such important feature was the restriction of the use of zoning to metropolitan, or at least urban centers. In these densely populated, functionally heterogeneous areas the potential for harmful effects from the interaction of various land uses was great. At the same time, the spatial separation of land uses must generally have been achievable at relatively low cost. It is thus no accident that zoning was first used in these areas.

In the open country, external effects have been much less pronounced, and while it is difficult to speculate about the costs of zoning

3. Instead of speaking of a "reduction" of technological external diseconomies, it would be more precise to speak of the elimination of Pareto-relevant externalities. Even at a Pareto optimum, externalities remain. Only Pareto-relevant externalities have been eliminated. For a discussion of this point and the concept of externalities see Buchanan and Stubblebine (1962).

in rural areas, it is doubtful that the costs are sufficiently low to justify zoning there on the basis of externality reductions. Since the benefits derived from the avoidance of externalities in rural areas are likely to be smaller than in urban places, zoning would, of course, be justified only if its costs were lower in the former than in the latter.

In Chapter 5, available studies on the effectiveness of zoning are reviewed. While it may be appropriate to seek the primary rationale for a direct regulatory device such as zoning in its effectiveness in reducing the types of negative external effects under consideration here, the economic benefits of zoning may be broader. It may also contribute to the other two objectives specified above: public goods supply and cost minimization in the provision of public services. For this reason, in part, the studies reviewed below did not focus on the effectiveness of zoning in externality reduction per se. Instead, they analyzed primarily its effects on property values and the spatial distribution of land uses. Moreover, zoning as a land use control technique must also be evaluated from the standpoint of equity and political acceptability.

Can the analysis of externality reduction in land use through public policy be carried a bit further? Until now we have talked only about zoning. Most planners readily point out that zoning is only an administrative tool useful for implementing the "comprehensive plan." The latter and the activities necessary to formulate it should be the primary targets of both public scrutiny and the planners' professional inputs.[4] Yet, in practice, the characteristics of plans are discussed in terms of R-4s and C-1s (the language of zoning) and not in terms of the fundamental conflicts among land use objectives that planning is to resolve.

The focus of comprehensive planning through zoning on such standards as minimum lot sizes and spatial homogeneity in land use is very significant. Such standards are thought to be related to the occurrence of negative external effects. But how closely are the requirements set by current land use plans actually related to externality reduction?

Perhaps we can use an analogy from environmental economics where externality abatement is, of course, the primary policy objective. It has been shown (Clark 1972) that policy, to be most effective, must be directed as specifically as possible to the external effect. Measurement and administrative problems aside, if we wish to reduce water pollution, a tax on fertilizer residues in return flows from irrigation would be more effective than a tax on either fertilizer or the crop to which the fertilizer is applied. We may generally assume that the

---

4. The distinction between the comprehensive plan and the zoning ordinance has been the subject of a recent court decision in Oregon (Baker vs. Milwaukie).

larger the number of physical and social–behavioral relationships between the policy variable and the externality output, the less effective the policy. How does zoning rate in this regard?

Zoning seeks to reduce such external effects as visual and air pollution, noise, traffic congestion, and groundwater pollution. The policy variable, spatial separation of land uses if often far removed from the external effects, and many complex technological and social–behavioral relationships are involved. The effectiveness of zoning in externality reduction is difficult to assess because of the indirect relationship between land use per se and the externality.

In the long run, another effect of zoning may be more important: its failure to provide incentives for technological and institutional innovations that reduce the social costs of externalities. Take, for example, our insistence on low-density residential settlements in the open country to maintain groundwater quality. Such zoning is predicated upon the use of septic tanks to handle domestic wastes. Given low-density zoning, septic tanks become, in fact, the optimal waste disposal system. No incentives are provided for developing a waste disposal technology less demanding of the waste absorptive capacity of land and hence more likely to reduce the external effects.

With standard setting of this type, there are likely to be additional difficulties. First, there is no explicit accounting for the costs involved in setting standards at a certain level. For example, larger minimum lot-size requirements make new residences more expensive, increase the amount of land demanded for residential purposes, and further exacerbate the competition between residential and other land uses. Second, because there is a less than one-to-one correspondence between the standard and the externality, other unintended and undesirable effects may result from the standard. In the example of large-lot requirements, higher costs for residential lots may make the neighborhoods where they are applied more exclusive by income class.

There is hope that the whole concept of zoning may eventually change to a system where functionally heterogeneous land uses are grouped together if their "performance characteristics" are consistent. Land use control by "performance standards" is the suggested approach (Horack 1952, Stockham 1974). Stockham provides some encouraging evidence of increasing acceptance of performance standards. Central to this approach is to focus as closely as possible on phenomena giving rise to external effects. Criteria currently being considered include emission levels, traffic generation, development intensity, visual performance, economic impact, and performance related to land capability. Planning based on such criteria would provide incentives for the modification of the socially objectionable characteristics of certain land uses. Nor would it require that all different land uses be spatially separated. A district would encompass several uses and would be differentiated from other districts on the basis of performance criteria. Hence, it would also be possible to obtain the social benefits that should flow from neighborhoods functionally more heterogeneous than those we currently observe.

PROVISION OF PUBLIC GOODS

Rationales other than the existence of external effects as discussed above support public intervention in land use, particularly in non-urban areas. Public goods or the need to provide them, furnish another justification. Although this section focuses primarily on public goods (objective 2 above), a brief comment on the third objective is in order to avoid confusion in terminology. The third economic efficiency goal is the reduction of costs in the provision of public services. It is necessary here to draw a distinction between public goods and public services.

The principal characteristic of public goods is that one person's consumption of them does not diminish the quantity left for others. In the land use area, an attractive view or certain services of parks are examples of public goods. They are available for consumption by everyone at the same level and hence may also be thought of as joint-consumption goods. This does not mean, however, that everyone necessarily values their consumption equally.

Another characteristic of public goods is a degree of simultaneity in their consumption. They can always be consumed by more than one user at the same time: many individuals can simultaneously enjoy an attractive view, a public park, or the protection of the police.

The joint-consumption nature of public goods typically makes it impossible to provide them efficiently through private markets. If such goods have strictly "public" characteristics, one person's consumption of them would not diminish the quantity left for others to consume. Since the first person's consumption would require no sacrifice from others, the only price which would not misallocate consumption of the good would be zero. Obviously, such a price would not draw private resources into the production of public goods. Hence, the provision of public goods generally entails some type of government action.

Public services, on the other hand, subsumes all goods and services provided by the public sector. They have something in common with public goods such as difficulties with private market provision, and some public services have important public goods characteristics. But most, if not all, public services also provide *private* goods: my drinking water is not yours, even if it flows through the same publicly provided pipeline. One difference between public goods and public services is that, at least in principle, an individual's consumption of a public service is measurable. Consumption is by the individual, at a level determined by him, not jointly. Because of this latter characteristic some of these usually public services are at times supplied by private companies.

Another distinguishing characteristic of public services is that they are frequently produced under conditions of declining average costs. As with public goods, setting prices equal to marginal costs will not attract sufficient resources into their production. For example, if sewage collection and treatment services were priced equal to their marginal costs, the revenues collected would be insufficient to amortize the investment in these facilities.

We argue here that somewhat different policies may be required for the optimal provision of public goods as contrasted with the efficient production of public services. We shall concentrate first on the former, giving brief attention to zoning. Later chapters also will scrutinize various land use planning measures for their efficiency in providing public goods.

One must recognize the difficulty of generalizing about efficiency aspects of providing public goods through zoning; the kinds of public goods vary widely. One important characteristic must be the "publicness" of the good. Take, for example, an ecologically important area whose preservation might be desired to maintain a unique biological community for scientific study. The expected benefits would accrue mainly to future generations and might be globally distributed. Near the other extreme is the nondevelopment of a hayfield in the midst of housing developments. Its open-space value would be capitalized into the value of neighboring properties, and the benefits would be immediate and accrue to a relatively small and well-defined public.

To use zoning to keep both the ecologically important area and the hayfield from more intensive development is to treat two very different situations alike. In each case the burden of the provision of the public good falls on the property owner, who is precluded from realizing potential development opportunities. If the parcels of land were in public ownership, the public decision-maker would have at least some incentives to weigh the benefits and costs of development. In all of the other cases where traditional zoning is used, there are fewer incentives to weigh the costs as well as the benefits in the preservation decision. On the basis of the underlying incentive system, one would expect to find many instances in which the preference for the public good is generally overstated when it is to be provided through zoning.

Public investment may be a much better tool for public goods provision than zoning, especially if the investment is made by the "relevant public": those who will enjoy the goods. Of course, this approach would not solve the problems connected with unrevealed preferences. Possible a multitude of "special service districts," could be developed but their administrative costs could be high. Indeed, the costs of organizing them might be so high that many such organizations necessary to provide public goods would not be formed. Still, the inefficiencies associated with the current system are sufficiently large that at least some experimentation with an alternative is in order.

Several suggestions for alternatives have been made. An ad valorem tax on adjoining properties has been proposed (McMillan 1973) as a source of funds with which the public might purchase land for open-space uses. Various schemes based on transferable development rights (TDRs) can be interpreted as attempts to shift the burdens of open-space provision to a larger base. (TDRs are the subject of a later chapter.) Preferential taxation of farm land has been employed to reduce the rate of transfer of agricultural land to more intensive uses (Gustafson and Wallace 1975, Barron and Thompson 1973). Compensable zoning has been suggested in Oregon as a means of addressing equity problems created by traditional zoning (Committee on Environment and Land Use 1973). Zoning auctions are still another way of trying to achieve the same objective (Clawson 1971, p. 346).

Preservation of open space is not the only land use goal with public goods characteristics. The preservation of prime agricultural land is another topic we are inclined to classify in the "public goods" category. If its goal is the maintenance of an agricultural production potential, it definitely has public goods aspects.

A public policy of preserving agricultural land to maintain an agricultural potential assumes a limited cropland base on the one hand and a direct relationship between the amount of land currently in cultivation and agricultural output on the other. This observation may be too simplistic: much of the world's arable land remains untilled and future additions to the cropland base are possible. Historically, there are also many examples of expanding agricultural output from a fixed cropland base. Such increases were brought about mainly by improvements in non-land inputs such as mechanical, chemical, and biological technology (Carter et al. 1975, pp. 51–55).

There is, of course, no reason to be complacent about future needs to increase agricultural output or about protecting ourselves from various disasters that might affect agricultural production. But one must wonder if the emphasis on land is not misplaced. It may be that the availability of energy is more important for the maintenance of agricultural output than is the number of acres in production. Furthermore, in terms of avoiding or minimizing the effects of catastrophic events and bringing about further improvements in agricultural production, society may gain as much from investments in understanding the natural and socioeconomic forces in food production as it would from foregoing some opportunities to put land now in agriculture to alternative uses. The argument is at least suggested that the maintenance of an agricultural potential to supply food for an increasing world population is only marginally related to land use planning issues in the United States.

A local community may have other, more compelling reasons to maintain its land in agriculture. Locally and in the short run the relationship between the number of acres in cultivation and the quantity of agricultural output is much closer than it is from the global and longer-run perspective. A community may benefit from a more diversified economy by maintaining its farming sector, and problems of unused capacity in agricultural processing and supply sectors of the local economy may be avoided by maintaining stability in the level of agricultural activity.

The final argument may be still more meritorious. It relates to the need to reduce the conversion of land from open-space uses and maintain greater land use flexibility. Many land use conversions may become economically irreversible even though the uses to which the land has been converted become suboptimal as economic circumstances change. The costs to society, perhaps into perpetuity, of living with the suboptimal land use may be many times greater than those of maintaining flexibility. To achieve the latter it might have been necessary only to forego some minor, short-run developmental opportunities.

Although the maintenance of land use flexibility, as well as food production potential have public goods characteristics, they certainly are not pure public goods. If the land area in agricultural use becomes the predominant constraint on agricultural output, the shares of total returns flowing to landowners will increase. Similarly, if the value of the benefits of developing land now is less than that of developing it later, a private landowner will rationally postpone development. This is not to make light of important reasons why the private decision-maker's calculus may not reach the socially optimal conversion rate, but even superficial analysis indicates that many of the factors responsible for divergence between the private and the socially optimal rates of land conversion are policy variables. They relate to taxation policies and how the costs of extending important public services are borne.

REDUCING COSTS OF PROVIDING PUBLIC SERVICES

The final major economic efficiency rationale for public intervention in land use decision-making relates to the costs of public provision of services. This may be the argument most frequently used, especially for the control of residential development in rural areas. Indeed, some reflection about the urbanization of almost any rural area near a major urban center suggests some hypotheses about possible cost savings in the provision of public services given a settlement pattern other than the prevailing one. A recent major study does precisely this, it constructs synthetic cost functions for the extension of some important public services given various residential densities (Real Estate Research Corporation 1974).

There is an extensive literature on the empirical determination of the costs of providing public services which needs to be analyzed to see what light it sheds on how cost differences in public service provision are related to the spatial distribution of relatively low density residential land uses in rural or rural–urban fringe areas. It is not sufficient to assume that such cost differences are associated with settlement patterns. For public policy purposes it is necessary to know the magnitude of these variations and the variables responsible for them.

The important policy issue in this area is likely to be the pricing of public services to the consumer. There are important parallels between this case and the two discussed above. Again, inefficiencies are likely to be associated with a pricing system which divorces payment by the beneficiary from the costs of providing the service. Certain developments may appear less costly to those responsible for creating them than they actually are because some of the costs are borne by others. Pricing is a broader issue than simply minimizing local government outlays for public services, however constrained local budgets may be.

Let us assume that the costs of extending public services to a subdivision farther removed from centrally available facilities were higher than those of extending them to a subdivision closer to the center. Simple cost minimization would insist on placing the subdivision at the closer location, regardless of how beneficial the more distant location otherwise might be. If instead, a pricing system were used which caused developers to take into account all costs directly associated with the decision to place a subdivision in one location or another, these costs could be compared with the corresponding benefits from residents' locational preference pattern and an efficient choice could be made.

Greater reliance on some "marginal cost pricing" scheme affords the significant advantage of incorporating the consumer's evaluation of residential choice into the decision framework. The only commonly employed alternative to such a "marginal cost pricing" scheme is zoning, but planners find it difficult to obtain efficiency benefits with this tool similar to those achieved through greater reliance on consumers' own evaluations. In drawing zone boundaries, planners would have to weigh this criterion as well as the others discussed earlier, but there would be no opportunity to gain the informational advantages the consumer has in making his location choice. It would hence be necessary to derive benefit as well as cost functions for various residential patterns. These are very difficult assignments.[5] We should not expect planners to be able to make such evaluations in the near future.

Our emphasis here lies on passing along to the consumer the cost differences related to the settlement pattern or, more simply, to the locational aspects of land use. There are other important issues in the pricing of public services, but they are not germane to land use planning although land use planning institutions are often the forums where they are discussed. We refer here to what economists call the "declining average cost curve problem" discussed above. This phenomenon prevails with many public services and provides the rationale for public supply of many such services and for regulation of public utilities. As in the case of public goods we have a situation where charging the social marginal costs for the consumption of a service does not create enough revenue to support the service. For example, when the marginal cost of supplying sewage treatment service to an additional residence is zero, given existing facilities, the marginal-cost pricing rule requires a zero charge to the residence. Hence, the residence would make no contribution to amortizing the cost of the treatment plant. Thus, local governments find it difficult to finance sewage treatment and similar facilities. To support these services they either draw upon other resources or attempt to raise some revenues through user charges that are not marginal cost oriented.

We expect that this problem has much to do with controversies concerning growth in many communities. Note that it is not a location-related problem. At least in principle, it would be possible to reflect location-related cost differences in public service charges. The problem here is more complex and concerns the method of financing additions to public service capacities. The physical location of the cause of the additional need is irrelevant.

The controversy in Corvallis, Oregon over the location of a new plant of the Hewlett–Packard Company may illustrate this problem. The plant site, almost adjacent to the city's waste treatment plant, could hardly be more advantageous from the standpoint of minimizing the costs of water supply and disposal. The company reportedly agreed to compensate the city for all variable costs of making these services available. Still, those who opposed the plant's location in Corvallis may

---

5. A limited effort to model residential choice has just been completed at Oregon State University (Schefter 1976).

have had a valid argument in pointing out that Hewlett–Packard's move would hasten the day when the capacity of the city's waterworks would be exhausted and lead to capital costs for new construction which would not be borne by Hewlett–Packard alone. Although such a problem, created by the "lumpiness" in the costs of providing certain public services (which has nothing to do with settlement patterns) is no less important than the problem of location-related differences in the marginal costs of providing certain public services, it is clear that zoning can address itself only to location-related factors. The pricing of public services can do more than that.

We have sketched three major efficiency criteria which appear relevant to land use decisions which (especially the first two) will be applied to the analysis of major land use planning techniques in Chapters 5 through 7. Before that we turn to a discussion of the distributional aspects of land use planning in Chapter 3 and an analysis of political acceptability in Chapter 4.

✳ *Chapter 3*

Distributive Effects of Land Use Control

The benefits and costs of any governmental regulation are often substantial and are seldom spread uniformly across the affected population. One should expect the implementation of any land use planning program to generate many benefits and costs distributed among many people.[1] Even assuming that a land use plan was designed to meet the efficiency criteria discussed in Chapter 2, there is no assurance whatsoever that such a plan would have a "desirable" distribution of impacts. A simple comparison of total benefits and costs is not enough. The question of *who receives the benefits and who incurs the costs is also vitally important.* This is primarily an issue of equity or fairness, but also has important ramifications for economic efficiency and political acceptability.[2]

We begin by discussing several dimensions of equity. A rationale for considering compensation and recapture is then developed, emphasizing the importance of compensation of losses and recapture of benefits in moving toward efficient land use control. The chapter concludes with a brief discussion of the distributive effects that may be expected from public regulation of land use and some partial evidence on the distribution of real estate among wealth classes.

1. Hagman (1974, 1975) provides an array of illuminating examples of potential benefits and costs attendant to many governmental problems that directly affect land use.
2. The political implications of the distribution of benefits and costs from land use control are treated in Chapter 4.

SOME DIMENSIONS OF EQUITY

The purpose of this section is modest: to identify three distinctions which can be used to organize or develop views of equity. Although many distinctions can be developed, only the three to be used in later analyses are introduced here.

Procedural and Allocative Dimensions

Views of equity may focus on either the impartiality of decision procedures or the fairness of the actual decisions. Emphasis on due process and equality of opportunity are examples of concerns for *procedural* equity. Views of equity that focus on the consequences of decisions have an *allocative* emphasis.

Allocations, of course, depend upon the decision procedures used, and surveying alternative decision procedures shows that the association between procedural equity and allocative equity is likely to be inverse. As will be discussed in Chapter 4, decision procedures open to all may yield allocations that systematically disadvantage certain groups. Allocative equity may require procedures that subsidize the participation of some, but not all participants.

Concerns for procedural equity seem to predominate in current land use control activities. "Timely notice," sequences of hearings, and appeal mechanisms emphasize procedures which can be defended as available and open to all citizens. With increasing public discussion of compensation mechanisms, however, concern for one aspect of allocative equity may be on the rise.

Individual or Categorical Dimensions

Views of equity may apply either to individuals or to categories of people. Philosophical systems are often most useful in identifying the equities or inequities experienced by individuals, and much of the concern for compensation or variance in land use controls focuses on individual landowners. Planning commissions, appeal boards, and courts of law are typically structured to *resolve* claims of inequities in land use controls on a case-by-case basis. However, public policy—to the extent that it tries to *promote* some concept of equity—seems capable only of handling crude categories of people: blacks and whites, men and women, families above and families below some poverty line, or veterans and nonveterans.

Dimensions Within or Between Categories

Views of equity may compare people within a category or people between categories. Where categories are ordinally related like income categories, one might refer to views of equity with horizontal or vertical applications. In land use most interest seems to be centered on equity within categories, e.g., among owners of undeveloped land about to be zoned either residential or agricultural. There does not appear to be a similarly strong focus on equity implications between such categories as landowner and potential homeowner.

WHY CONSIDER COMPENSATION AND RECAPTURE?

Efficiency

As explained in Chapter 2, the underlying rationale for employing efficiency criteria in land use planning is the ability of these criteria to identify land use problem areas where public intervention may reap "gains from trade": i.e., someone can be made better off without making anyone else worse off.[3] Since the use of these criteria stems from the failure of private market decisions to account for all benefits and costs, public intervention can be viewed as a necessary condition for achieving efficiency of land use allocations. However, it is fallacious to argue further that public intervention is sufficient to achieve efficient outcomes (Krutilla 1966).

Unless the techniques used to achieve land use control objectives incorporate some method of linking the costs of land use planning to those who correspondingly benefit, a less than efficient outcome can be expected. Without such techniques, pressures are set up for both those who benefit and those who suffer, to alter the efficient allocation of land uses desired. "Winners," those who benefit in excess of what they pay, will demand the goods and services excessively and may exert political pressure for expanded supply. "Losers," on the other hand, will push in any way possible for reduced or eliminated supply, since they absorb a disproportionately high share of the costs. Compensating losses from recaptured gains in land use planning may therefore aid in securing efficient outcomes.[4]

3. A comprehensive discussion of the reasons for considering compensation and recapture of losses and benefits from public regulation of land use would include a discussion of legal precedents for doing so. However, since this study focuses on economic rationale, it will not address the legal precedents which constrain or permit compensation and recapture. For an extensive review of the literature dealing with betterment recapture and worsement avoidance techniques related to public regulation of land use, see Lowenberg et al. (1974). For a new approach to the legal arguments surrounding compensation, an excellent exposition is Costonis (1975). Another good legal reference to the "taking" dilemma in land use control is Bosselman, Callies, and Banta (1973). Some of the political dimensions of compensation and recapture will be addressed in Chapter 4.

4. The reader familiar with economic welfare analysis will note that advocacy of this compensation/recapture argument is tantamount to accepting the distribution of prop-

Consider the example in Chapter 2 of determining the efficient use of an agricultural meadow surrounded by residential property. Ignoring spillovers or external effects, the meadow's owner has an incentive to sell or use the meadow for the highest valued opportunity. On the other hand, the residential property owners, considering the prospect of a shopping center in their neighborhood leading to lower property values for their homes, have an incentive to secure public designation of the meadow as permanent open space. Faced with a requirement for compensation and recapture of land value changes due to the public action, the owners of both the meadow and the residential property could be expected to reconsider their initial positions. Given compensation and recapture requirements, property owners who stand to gain or lose from a land use decision should be less inclined to exert pressure on land use planning bodies than they are under direct regulation.[5]

There is no guarantee that the ultimate use designated for the meadow will be efficient, i.e., the windfalls will exceed the wipeouts, since that decision is a public choice based on *expectations* of net social benefits. In practice, full taxation of the benefits and compensation for the losses resulting from public control of land use faces both conceptual and operational problems. Accurate identification of affected parties can be complicated. Many planning actions affect individuals or groups distant from a land use designation. On the meadow example some of the benefits of maintaining it as open space may be spread over the entire community, making compensation for or assessment of effects confined to the neighborhood less than ideal. Likewise, a commercial designation for the meadow may lower the value of all other commercial properties in the community. Measurement of the "true" gains and losses resulting from public action is also complicated. Reliance on market prices to establish changes in property values may not be adequate. The changed value of an affected landowner's property reflects the interaction of total market demand and supply influences, not necessarily the landowner's evaluation of the benefit or

---

erty rights in real estate prevailing before land use planning action. Since that distribution is probably highly correlated to the distribution of individual wealth, it could be argued that advocacy of compensation and recapture should remain a normative distribution concern. However, compensation and recapture based on the prevailing distribution of property rights in real estate to achieve efficient outcomes does not preclude lump-sum transfers afterward to achieve equity objectives.

5. Without provision for compensation and recapture, the estimation of benefits and costs often boils down to undocumented assertions attendant on the power struggle between those expecting to gain and those expecting to lose. Individuals not fortunate enough to forecast the effect on their own wealth or income position may not even be represented.

cost of the public action to him. Goods and services not traded in the marketplace, such as scenic beauty or low noise levels, require either objective approximation or subjective judgment of their money value.

Regardless of these problems, carefully planned and administered systems of compensation and recapture represent a potential improvement in efficiency over land use control through direct regulation without such provision. As an indication of this potential improvement, zoning by eminent domain (ZED) and transferable development rights (TDR) sytems which feature simultaneous compensation and recapture provisions have recently been proposed. Chapters 6 and 7 will examine each of these techniques.

Distribution of Benefits and Costs

Regardless of the potential role of compensation and recapture in aiding efficiency evaluations or securing efficient outcomes, the ultimate decision to make adjustments for changes in property value will rest on the social desirability of the distributive effects of land use control as viewed by public decision-makers. As shown in Chapter 2, each set of rules for the distribution and use of property leads to an outcome. Not all are efficient, but there are an infinite number of efficient allocations, all different with respect to the distribution of wealth and income to individual members of society.

The economic welfare of society therefore depends upon satisfying efficiency conditions *and* meeting social goals with respect to the distribution of goods and services among individuals. Indeed, it can be shown that under certain conditions moving from an efficient to an inefficient allocation may be socially preferable on the basis of society's distributive preferences. These distributive preferences are formed by social values which determine what is "equitable." As discussed above, the dimensions of equity are many, and the perceived equity of the distributive effects of land use control may therefore vary from one individual to another. Some people may place greater importance on procedural safeguards in a land use control system (e.g., zoning variance procedures) than on allocative outcomes (e.g., the influences on affected parties' wealth and income levels). Some may be concerned that individuals be treated "fairly," either procedurally or allocatively, while others may focus on the disadvantaging of particular groups of categories (e.g., nonlandowners). Finally, "fair" distributive effects of land use control within certain categories *or* between certain categories may present two additional equity dimensions. However, before establishing the "equity" of any distributive effects of land use control on any basis, it is necessary to identify these effects.

IDENTIFYING POTENTIAL DISTRIBUTIVE
EFFECTS OF LAND USE CONTROL

In terms of allocative equity it is useful to distinguish between two types of distributive effects, specific and general. Specific distributive effects refer to changes in the wealth or income of individuals because of their ownership or use of properties directly influenced by land use regulations. For example, rezoning a piece of land from a lower to a higher intensity of use (e.g., residential to commercial) may increase its market value and the owner's wealth. General distributive effects include those which change the wealth or income of different groups of people, irrespective of the specific spatial incidence of land use regulations. Restrictions which reduce the amount of land available for a particular use (e.g., multiple family residences) and thereby increase development costs for that use are appropriate examples. These two types of distributive effect are not unrelated, since the occurrence of a specific effect—preserving the agricultural land of certain farmers on the urban fringe—could cause a general effect—increased cost of housing for new residents.

Specific Effects

Implementation of any comprehensive land use plan will ultimately require that certain restrictions apply to each land parcel in the regulated area, thereby defining its intensity of use. Traditionally, zoning regulations have been used for this purpose. The regulated area is divided into various land use districts, e.g., residential, commercial, industrial. Within each district other regulations apply to such development characteristics as lot areas, setback requirements, height, size, and use of buildings, and density of population. Often the cumulative effect of all these restrictions significantly influences the value of a land parcel and/or adjoining property. If a new comprehensive land use plan allows one person to sell his lot (formerly zoned residential) for a service station, his wealth may increase while the value of adjoining or nearby residential land decreases. Regardless of zoning regulations, certain properties will be more valuable than others because of locational factors (e.g., distance to urban center, transportation networks, and physical characteristics of the land), but, zoning regulations can also be an important determinant of value. As Muller states, "The most valuable and probably most controversial, implicit grant by the public sector is based on the legal power of county or municipal government to approve a change of land use from less intensive to more intensive development" (1972, pp. 227).

Any comprehensive land use planning program that entails zoning regulations for all land parcels will bring about many specific distributive effects. The important question concerns the incidence of specific benefits or specific costs caused by land use controls with respect to income and wealth classes. If the specific effects are randomly distributed, the decision-maker determining land use policy may not be concerned; but if wealthier classes receive the specific benefits while poorer classes bear the specific costs, or vice versa, he may have justification for concern.

Is there any way to relate the incidence of specific benefits and costs to groups of people rather than analyze each individual impact? This is possible only when a group of landowners or landusers are similarly affected by land use control. Land use control on the urban fringe again provides an example. Suppose a municipality desires to stop all development in one direction and preserve open space and "prime" agricultural land. To achieve this purpose, it restricts a block of land held by many landowners from being sold for development. Each landowner has been affected in a like manner. Information regarding the income and wealth positions of these landowners could be an important input for the decision-making process of land use control. Unfortunately this type of analysis cannot be generalized over different zoning jurisdictions, since the assessment of specific distributive effects depends on the basic nature of the land use plan, i.e., regulatory objectives and their spatial incidence.

General Effects

Although specific distributive effects may be the most visible impacts of land use control, aggregate parameters, such as average prices of land and housing and even levels of employment and income, may also be affected over time. Since these aggregate parameters are also influenced by many other factors, differentiating the influence of land use control is fraught with problems. To complicate the distributive assessment further, the occurrence and magnitude of general distributive effects must be related to such equity constructs as the relative income or wealth levels of affected parties.

To ascertain the impact on equity of distributive effects from changes in the price of real estate, it would be necessary first to describe the current distribution of real estate ownership for income or wealth classes. Although this information does not directly identify the distributive impact of land use controls, it provides a necessary benchmark data source that can be related to land use control effects so that policy-makers dealing with land use control can more effectively gauge the "fairness" of land use control policies.

Some partial evidence on the distribution of real estate ownership by wealth classes is provided by a recent study. Based on real estate investment theory, Erlandson (1976) proposed that the proportion of an individual's wealth devoted to home real estate is inversely related to his wealth level while the proportion devoted to business (farm and nonfarm) and speculative real estate is directly related.[6] Table 3.1 presents data from a national sample of individual financial characteristics used to statistically test the strength of each hypothesized relationship in the Erlandson study. The statistical results added considerable support for each expectation. Although the amount invested in home real estate increases with successively higher income classes (column 3), investment in home real estate as a proportion of wealth declines.[7] Overall, consumer units held a greater proportion of their wealth in home real estate, 27% (column 6), than in any other asset form covered by the data.

Business real estate, as examined in the same study, represented an increasing proportion of total wealth up to the $25,000 income class and a decreasing proportion above that. Even though one would expect a small proportion of consumer units to have incomes over $25,000 in 1962, the statistical results do not strictly conform to the business real estate hypothesis. Reflection suggests that investors earning more than $25,000 in 1962 may have turned to non–real estate investments because of the greater opportunity costs for time necessary to make real estate investments. Column 10 of Table 3.1 indicates that the proportion of wealth in publicly traded stocks increased at an increasing rate for wealth levels above those corresponding to a $25,000 annual income. This evidence is consistent with the alternative explanation.[8]

6. Four areas of real estate investment theory were analyzed to derive these propositions (Erlandson 1976, pp. 7–33). First, the different objectives—use, regular return, and capital gain—of real estate investors were explored. Second, the characteristics of real estate which provide special incentives—cash flow, tax shelter, and sale proceeds—and disincentives—risks related to financing, purchasing power, and liquidity—were analyzed. Next, special characteristics of financing real estate ownership—leverage, mortgage lender objectives, and mortgage insurance and guarantee programs—were related to income and wealth levels. Finally, the dimensions of the investor's financial position—assets, earning capacity, and liabilities—were treated. After an exploration of each of the four general areas, the investment advantages and disadvantages of each form of real estate—home, business, and speculative—were summarized to provide the basis for each hypothesis.

7. Although strictly comparable data were not available for years after 1962, information taken from *Statistics of Income* (1972) indicated that home real estate constituted a smaller proportion of income (rather than wealth) at successively higher income classes. These results can be viewed as supplementary to the primary test and supporting evidence for the hypothesis since income and wealth are directly correlated.

8. It should also be noted that the data used for this test did not include corporate holdings of real estate, and therefore business and speculative real estate holdings by investors in higher income classes may be understated.

Table 3-1. Mean Level of Equity in Specified Forms of Real Estate and Publicly Traded Stock for All Consumer Units, by 1962 Income

1	2	3	4	5	6	7	8	9	10
		Specific Real Estate Forms						*Publicly*	
1962 Income	*Wealth*	*Home*	*Business*	*Speculative*	*Column (3) ÷ (2)*	*Column (4) ÷ (2)*	*Column (5) ÷ (2)*	*Traded Stock*	*Column (9) ÷ (2)*
$ 0– 2,999	$ 7,609	$ 3,204	$ 1,454	$ 300	.421	.191	.039	$ 450	.059
3,000– 4,999	10,025	3,390	1,261	995	.338	.126	.099	686	.068
5,000– 7,499	13,207	4,495	2,286	860	.340	.173	.065	1,402	.106
7,500– 9,999	19,131	7,075	2,279	1,842	.370	.119	.096	2,659	.139
10,000–14,999	28,021	9,566	4,287	1,905	.341	.153	.068	4,521	.161
15,000–24,999	62,966	15,053	10,229	6,358	.239	.162	.101	10,431	.166
25,000–49,999	291,317	32,528	61,986	30,178	.112	.213	.103	71,368	.245
50,000–99,999	653,223	38,298	277,383	19,691	.059	.425	.030	161,765	.248
100,000 and over	1,698,021	88,248	286,732	50,520	.052	.169	.030	956,339	.563
All consumer units	*20,982*	*5,653*	*3,881*	*1,572*	*.269*	*.185*	*.075*	*3,724*	*.177*

Source: Erlandson (1976, p. 40), based on Projector and Weiss, SFCC 1966, Tables A-8 and A-10.

Like those for business real estate the statistical results for speculative real estate showed the proportion of total wealth invested increasing up to the $25,000 income level and decreasing above that point. Again, even though the percentage of total consumer units with an annual income over $25,000 in 1962 is expected to be quite small, the statistical results are at variance with the speculative real estate hypothesis. A partial explanation for this may be that the data used did not include speculative real estate holdings of corporations in which individuals owned stock. Stock ownership should increase with income class level because the management costs borne by the individual for investing in corporate stock are lower than those for speculative land and building investments.[9] Data from Table 3.1 (column 8) also indicate that speculative real estate represented less than 10% of total wealth for all consumer units, the lowest of the three types of real estate.

To describe the relationship between real estate ownership and income class more completely, Erlandson also analyzed the relative frequency of home, business, and speculative real estate ownership by income class using data from the *Survey of Consumer Finances* (1962, 1970) and the *Survey of Financial Characteristics of Consumers (SFCC)* (1962) (see Table 3.2 for sample data). Results indicated that home real estate ownership is widely diffused throughout the population, varying from 40% of all consumer units in the lowest income class to 96% in the highest (SFCC, 1962). Business real estate ownership, on the other hand, is less widely diffused and is characterized by a lower relative frequency within all income classes (especially the lower ones) and an apparent concentration in the middle to upper income classes. The frequency of speculative real estate ownership is even less widely diffused, being lower in all but two income classes and highly concentrated in the middle to upper income classes.

The Erlandson analysis used the latest available data, which nevertheless are not very current. Yet it may provide some indication of basic or stable relationships between forms of real estate ownership and income and wealth classes. Some examples illustrate the usefulness of these results in assessing the distributive impacts of land use controls.

Assume first that increased public control over land use increases the cost of home real estate—land and/or structures. We know from the frequency-of-ownership data (Table 3.2, column 2) that over one-half of all consumer units at all wealth levels will probably be affected. We also know that the greatest degree of wealth increase will occur among

9. See note 8.

Table 3–2. Percentage of Consumer Units Owning Specific Forms of Real Estate, by Income Class

(1) *1962 Income*	(2) *Home Real Estate*	(3) *Business (Farm and Nonfarm) Real Estate*	(4) *Speculative Real Estate*
$ 0– 2,999	40%	12%	5%
3,000– 4,999	45	12	7
5,000– 7,499	60	17	10
7,500– 9,999	73	18	18
10,000–14,999	80	22	18
15,000–24,999	86	26	29
25,000–49,999	92	64	36
50,000–99,999	94	70	36
100,000 and over	96	35	29
All consumer units	*57%*	*17%*	*11%*

SOURCE: Erlandson (1976, p. 57), based on Projector and Weiss, SFCC 1966, Tables A-8 and A-10.

those with low income or wealth levels who already own homes (Table 3.1, column 6). The increased cost of home real estate, will, however, simultaneously place the greatest burden on those with low wealth and income levels who plan to purchase homes. In essence, the increased cost of home real estate caused by land use control will transfer wealth from those who want to purchase homes (e.g., young people or migrants into the regulated area) to those who already own homes or home real estate (e.g., older people, home builders, and developers) especially to those owning more valuable homes. If land use control decreased the cost of home real estate, the effects would be reversed and favor those on the lower end of the income distribution who wish to purchase homes.

Second, assume that land use control increases the cost of business and speculative real estate. We know that the specific effects will probably be less widespread than for home real estate (Table 3.2, columns 3 and 4) and that their initial incidence and magnitude will fall more heavily on the higher income and wealth classes (Table 3.1, columns 7 and 8). For example, lowering the supply of new commercial building space may increase the price of existing units and thus benefit owners while increasing the costs to renters. We know that since owners are business real estate investors, there is a greater chance that they are from the middle and upper income classes (Table 3.2, column 3). Whether these higher costs of business can be passed on to consumers of the goods and services produced or sold in the commercial buildings depends upon the competitiveness of the markets for these goods and services and the occurrence of similar zoning actions in other market areas.

SUMMARY

These examples are only simple illustrations. Moreover, the distributive effects mentioned are only the most obvious of "first-round" influences. The actual distributive effects of land use control are much more diverse, consisting not only of "first-round" effects like changes in the income and wealth levels of real estate owners but also of "second-round" effects like influences on the income of local merchants caused by restricting the location of industrial activity. A comprehensive assessment of all the distributive effects of land use control would probably be too costly, but serious further study of the most obvious effects seems warranted. This may not only help to avoid an "undesirable" distribution of impacts from land use control but also indirectly aid in assessing the economic efficiency of land use control.

Chapter 4

Sociopolitical Constraints on Land Use Policies

INTRODUCTION

The previous chapters suggest that efficiency and equity constitute (or should constitute) two broad goals for land use planning. Economics has developed techniques for evaluating the efficiency of social institutions, and philosophy, and other disciplines have suggested means for evaluating and improving social justice. If, however, past performance in land use policy is a reasonable guide to future actions, neither the efficiency prescribed by the economist nor the equity procedures suggested by the philosopher will be implemented by the political system. Economists, philosophers, and land use planners will continue to find their desires frustrated by the refusal of the political process to adopt "better" land use policies.

In this chapter we attempt to explain the recalcitrance of political decision-makers. The planner, economist, or philosopher may attribute the lack of responsiveness of public officials to many causes. We suggest that constraints placed on the political decision process by social norms, political inequality among citizens, and institutionalized working rules produce the major discrepancies between public policies and the proposals of the economist, philosopher, or planner.

Most political decisions involve a distribution of rewards and deprivations—i.e., there are winners and losers. Rarely are there only winners. Depending on how individuals perceive their gains or losses and on their political resources and interests, those affected by a decision can be expected to allocate credit or blame and reward or punish the decision-maker. Thus, just as the political decision-maker allocates benefits and costs, he is in turn allocated the same. This reality for political decision-makers often leads to significant deviations from the social efficiency and equity prescribed by the economist, philosopher, or planner.

How "What is" Becomes "What is Right"

As noted in Chapters 2 and 3, the distribution of rights in society is closely intertwined with efficiency. Their current distribution partially reflects prevailing social norms concerning what is fair and just; and, as these norms change, legally protected rights will also change. For example, in past years many, if not most, persons accepted that paying a woman less than a man for equal work and giving preference to men in employment was fair. The presumed role of the man as primary provider for the family furnished one justification for this discrimination. Men had a right—a property right if you will—to employment preference and higher pay. Schools, the media, and other institutions that socialize individuals into various roles buttressed these norms and associated rights by stereotyping certain roles as male or female. The women's rights movement and associated ideas of justice such as equal pay for equal work challenged this notion of equity. Recent textbooks, TV programs, and other media reflect this challenge. Changing norms and social institutions changed public policy and redistributed rights to occupational and social roles between men and women.

This example demonstrates how under two different sets of rights and social norms (prior privilege for men yielding to greater equality between the sexes) an analysis such as that presented here would lead to two different groups of policy suggestions for achieving the highest level of social efficiency. Although efficiency, as defined in Chapter 2, can be improved if all benefits and costs have not been accounted for in the existing efficiency calculation, when society changed the value placed on women staying home and the role separation between men and women, what were once considered benefits came to be seen as costs. As norms and conceptions of equity change, social efficiency also changes. Rights and, therefore, efficiency are partially the products of social norms which in turn reflect dominant concepts of distributive equity and justice. However, as sociologists are fond of telling us (and empirical research throughout the social sciences has supported their claims), social norms, values, and conceptions of justice and equity are themselves partially products of the existing distribution of rights, duties, and privileges. Individuals growing up in a capitalist economy tend to see capitalism as equitable and just, while individuals growing up in a socialistic economy are likely to see socialism as more just. Efficiency, equity, norms, rules, and the distribution of rights and resources interact in a dynamic socioeconomic system. The system rarely changes rapidly because most of its elements reinforce the others. Because rights cause and are caused by prevailing practices, and because practices influence and are influenced by norms, there is a strong tendency in all societies to see what is as what is right. Changes occur, but radical changes are rare.

Social Norms and Rights Associated with Real Property

Land use and associated property rights provide an excellent example of changes in values, norms, rights, and policy. The impetus for these changes comes from the increasing value to some citizens of environmental goods such as clean air and water, the preservation of open space and wilderness, and the maintaining of agricultural lands. The attainment of these goods often clashes with two sets of values that continue to be held by a large number of persons: (1) the liberty and security associated with real property; and (2) the right of and need for economic expansion.

The rights associated with property are among the most deeply held values in the United States. In the period immediately prior to the Declaration of Independence the phrase, "Life, Liberty, and Property," occurred frequently in the writings of Jefferson, Madison, and other's who played prominent roles in the independence movement and the establishment of the state and national governments. Property ownership was perceived as a means through which individual liberty could be secured. The right of property, particularly real property, continues to be a basic value in our society and continues to support and be supported by other deeply held values. Brewster (1959) has suggested that the work ethic, the enterprise creed, the creed of self-reliance, and the democratic creed have been the four dominant values in the United States. The ownership of real property, especially home ownership, is consistent with each of these values, and policies encouraging the ownership of property have had consistent support. Federal and state policies related to borrowing and taxing provide well-known examples of government action to support home ownership. They provide an unmatched opportunity for persons with moderate incomes to acquire an asset which appreciates in value while retiring their indebtedness with less valuable dollars (Castle and Rettig 1972). Because of the importance of real property and its widespread ownership, policies that might reduce the value or security of property and associated rights meet severe opposition.

The land use control techniques to be examined in subsequent chapters, as well as most of those that have been proposed elsewhere, require the reallocations of rights associated with real property. When such reallocations conflict with widely accepted values, the sociocultural environment can be expected to constrain many policy actions even though these actions might increase efficiency and equity. Further limitations on policy alternatives may be expected when reallocations of rights redistribute them from the more politically influential to the less and when the outcomes of a proposed reallocation are uncertain. We now examine these sociocultural and political constraints and how they can be expected to affect the political acceptability of proposed changes in land use control.

The Political Allocation of Rights

We define *rights* as the behavior permitted and protected by social institutions. Depending upon the right under consideration, relevant institutions range from the family to national or international organizations. Property rights become the uses—potential and practiced—allowed or guaranteed by social institutions.

Initially, one observes that when rights are defined in terms of behavior, they must be specified with reference to particular individuals or groups. Specifically, a right may not pertain to all, and social institutions may protect certain behavior only for certain individuals. Rights are not immutable, and the protection provided by social institutions may change. The rights of husbands and wives change as the institution of marriage changes. At one time a college student may have the right to use food stamps but after congressional action that right may vanish. Nor is such formal action by a legislature always necessary. Rights may change simply by changes in the selective enforcement of laws.

Most rights are supported by social institutions that have little to do with government. Although the rights someone exercises as a child or adult, husband or wife, Elk or Moose, Unitarian or Mormon, consumer or producer, and employer or employee are influenced by government, within broad limits, they are protected by other institutions such as the family, the fraternal or religious organization, the market, or the labor union. Government becomes involved when individuals dispute rights and the disputants do not accept the authority of nongovernmental institutions either because of different values (beliefs as to what is authoritative) or for strategic reasons.

Chapters 2 and 3 suggested that the goals of public land use controls should be to improve efficiency by reducing negative effects created by incompatible uses, to improve the supply of public goods, and to reduce the cost and/or improve the quality of public services. In addition, proposed land use controls and associated changes in rights should be evaluated on the basis of their effects on equity. The motivations of citizens to request government action (or inaction) in the control of land use are not, however, limited to these goals. There are strong incentives for some individuals or groups to gain new rights and material benefits by using the political process to restrict the rights of—or impose costs on—other individuals or groups. Groups already organized for political action have particularly strong incentives to use the regulatory aspects of government to impose costs on the unorganized (Lowi 1964, 1972).

Within the political process the question is usually not "Given the existing distribution of rights, what is the most efficient solution to the removal of external effects?" but "Who has what rights?" The political system is rarely asked "What is the optimal level of a public good?" but "What public goods should be supplied and who should pay for them?" In the provision of public services the political issue is not simply to minimize the total costs of public services but to allocate those costs in a politically acceptable manner. For example, it rarely troubles a citizen if the total cost of a service is greater than its value. If the costs can be shifted to other (or future) citizens, he will not be concerned about the minimization of total costs. Only if the cost of that service *to him* is greater than its value *to him* will the citizen tend to question efficiency.

In summary, the political decision-maker in land use is not typically concerned with the efficiency questions of interest to economists. He is, rather, constantly involved in disputes over the distribution of rights and goods. As the continual zoning hearings, injunctions, and such extremely disparate court decisions as Mt. Laurel and Petaluma indicate, the prior question of who has what right remains unresolved. Whenever a new land use tool is proposed on the grounds that it will lead to greater social efficiency, the political decision-maker and the political participants respond not to the social efficiency argument but to the impact the land use technique is expected to have on their rights and privileges both now and in future disputes. For this reason, when rights are in dispute, as they almost always are, the concept of social efficiency provides little assistance in predicting how a political system resolves land use disputes.

POLITICAL DECISIONS AND EQUITY

Although there are philosophical analyses of justice from Plato to Bentham to Rawls, attempts to use them for evaluation of policies have not been successful. While the reasons for this lack of success often lie in the theories of justice, a fundamental problem with using a theory of social justice or equity to evaluate policies comes from the orientation of the theories to individuals while public policies tend to deal with groups. Theories like those of Rawls are like scalpels while policies are like meat cleavers (Herman Daly [1971] has called policy "the invisible foot.") Because policies are oriented to groups or categories of persons, evaluating any policy on the basis of its fairness entails relaxing many of the assumptions of theories oriented to individuals and looking not only at effects on individuals but at effects upon classes of persons as well.

The Department of Health, Education and Welfare's attempts to use policy to correct discrimination on the basis of race or ethnic background is an example of the difficulty of using policies to achieve social justice. These policies were designed to facilitate equality by compensating for the previous disadvantaged position of certain minorities. Because *on the average* blacks and Chicanos experience greater social and educational disadvantages than whites, institutions are encouraged to use quotas in accepting them. These quotas, since they apply to group, not individuals, could lead to a situation where the child of a black physician is given preference over the child of a white migrant worker.

As a guide to equity, the judicial process reflects problems similar to those that theories of justice pose: the courts are oriented toward individuals while land use policies are oriented toward groups. Although precedents are set by individual cases, these precedents tend to be inconsistent not only over time but also at any given time in different sections of the country.[1] Beyond these difficulties, the judicial process may favor the "haves" over the "have nots" even more than the legislative and executive branches of government. Galanter [1974] has provided extensive documentation of the advantages possessed by persons who frequently participate in the judicial process over those who participate less often.

Perhaps the crucial aspect of equity as it affects the social and political acceptability of a particular land use policy or technique is that initial demands for equity—pervasive as they are in property rights disputes—express only the equity concepts and interests of those actively involved in the dispute. For this reason, to the extent that equity appeals affect governmental allocations of rights, the "equity" concepts considered are those most palatable to the participants in the dispute. In such a situation the political decision-maker may find that "equity" requires an allocation of rights to the participants from the nonparticipants. For example, in Petaluma both the city council

1. A comprehensive treatment of the inconsistencies of the courts is given by Bosselman, Callies, and Banta [1974].

and the courts took rights from potential residents and allocated them to current residents.

The position of the political system on equity is not entirely fluid, responding only to the interests and influences involved in a single case. Precedents are set. Constitutions are subject to many, but not all, interpretations. Thus, concepts of equity developed in earlier decisions affect subsequent resolutions. This occurs partly because individuals cannot adopt equity positions solely for the sake of immediate political expediency. Participants in a dispute will accept and maintain collective positions on equity disadvantageous for the decision at hand if they perceive one or more of these three conditions: (1) they anticipate that the current decision will lead to future successful claims for themselves; (2) they are uncertain about the nature of their future interests; (3) they are uncertain about their future political influence. In all three situations, participants may accept the compensation of others if, by so doing, they support a collective position on equity from which they expect to benefit in the future.

These three conditions suggest that collective positions on equity for a broad range of rights will be relatively clear and stable in a political system if participation is widespread and there is rough equality in political influence. Where participation is not widespread, collective positions on equity may still be clear and stable, but for a narrower set of rights; namely, those which significantly favor the regular, influential participants. In addition, collective positions on equity will be more stable when the issue involved relates closely to the basic social values held by most citizens even though their immediate political interests are not directly relevant to the issue. In the United States, the freedoms of speech, religion, and assembly are such values and, as indicated above, the rights of real property have historically been close to this level.[2]

PATTERNS OF PUBLIC PARTICIPATION AND POLITICAL OUTCOMES

We suggest in the previous section that political decision-makers often allocate benefits to participants in the political process at the expense of nonparticipants. To the extent that this allocation excludes or un-

2. The attachment to the freedoms of speech, religion, and assembly is held more strongly in the abstract than it is when related to a specific situation such as whether a communist can speak in a public school. These freedoms, like property rights, are more subject to social and political restraint than is often assumed. Nevertheless, they hold symbolic value, and their infringement is more subject to challenge in the courts than that of less dearly held freedoms (Prothro and Grigg 1960).

derestimates certain costs (those borne principally by nonparticipants) and overestimates some benefits (typically those provided to partici- pants), and policy is not optimal from an efficiency standpoint.[3]

Previous studies of political participation have consistently found that participation is directly associated with social status (Campbell et al. 1962, Milbrath 1965, Verba and Nie 1972). The advantages of upper status individuals are further accelerated by their greater membership and activity in social organizations (Verba and Nie 1972, p. 208). Because political resources are unevenly distributed and political ad- vantages tend to be associated with economic advantages, it can be hypothesized that land use policies disproportionally benefit the economically advantaged. The extent of this advantage, however, will vary significantly depending on the political arena in which land use decisions are made, the types of policies chosen, and the means by which the policies are implemented.

The decision to participate may reasonably be expected to vary with an individual's expected utility of participation, the expected utility being a function of the perceived costs and benefits of participatory action. Following Riker and Ordeshook (1968), we can calculate the expected utility of participation as follows:

$$R = (P \times B) + (D - C) \tag{4.1}$$

where

R = the expected utility of participation less the expected utility of not participating
P = the citizen's subjectively estimated probability that his participa- tion will affect the outcome,
B = the absolute value of the differential utility between policy options
D = the pleasure (or displeasure) a citizen derives from the act of participation
C = the subjectively estimated cost of participation (e.g., time, money, information).

More simply phrased, a citizen is more likely to participate if he feels that the decision is important and that he can make a difference, if he likes participating, and if the cost of participating is low.

Examining the determinants of participation $(P, B, D,$ and $C)$, we can easily understand why participation tends to increase with social status. P, the citizen's subjectively estimated probability that his par-

3. In Chapter 2 it was shown that an improvement can always be made when account has not been taken of some benefits or costs.

ticipation will affect the outcome, is related to his perception of his own effectiveness in politics, and it is not surprising that persons with higher socioeconomic status (SES) perceive themselves as more effective (Campbell et al. 1962, p. 479). In part, higher SES citizens have learned by experience that they are effective in politics, and, in part, *perceptions of effectiveness in social and economic spheres lead to expectations of effectiveness in the political sphere.*

B reflects the difference between the preferred policy decision and the alternative policy. For example, if the decision of a zoning hearing might lower the value of your home, B would equal the difference between the utility of the existing situation and the expected utility of the situation after the zoning change. P and B are multiplied because even if the utility difference between the existing situation and the expected situation after a zoning change were high, if you estimated that your attendance at the hearing would make no difference in the decision, then $(P \times B)$ would still equal zero and you would not attend the hearing (assuming C exceeds D).

D represents the influence of an individual's attitude toward the actual act of participation. For example, we cannot account for electoral participation on the basis that a citizen believes his vote will be the deciding *one*. Rather, voting makes people feel good because they have done their civic duty, receive approval from others, and get to express support for a political system. The magnitude of D can be expected to vary directly with SES. Since public education—as its earliest proponents argued—teaches concepts of civic duty, persons with higher levels of education are more likely to be conscientious about civic duty and to associate with peers whose approval depends—in part—on such behavior. Moreover, citizens who have acquired or maintained above average levels of wealth are likely to derive pleasure from supporting the existing political system, but for citizens who consider themselves deprived in wealth, an act supporting the political system may have negative utility.

When "more difficult" political acts, such as going to and speaking at public meetings or campaigning for particular candidates or issues are examined, the utility of the participatory act itself (D) may remain an important variable. These activities offer the participant the opportunity to meet with friends, to be entertained, and to enjoy such psychological rewards as feeling satisfied with himself. Whether the activity is a meeting of the League of Women Voters or the county Republican Party or a public hearing on a proposed zoning change, the social benefits to the individual often outweigh the ostensible purpose of the activity (Olson 1965). Although political participation has a high intrinsic utility for some persons, for others it is negative. They may feel embarrassed to speak at public meetings or have such negative attitudes toward the process that they do not wish to become involved.

Because higher-status individuals are more likely to be active members of social organizations—particularly organizations involved in political activities (Verba and Nie 1972, p. 208)—and because they tend to have the social skills necessary to participate, the utility of participation is likely to be much higher for the more advantaged. For the less educated the chances of embarrassment or "feeling out of place" can be expected to be greater.

Because of the diminishing marginal utility of money, some participation costs (C) are lower for higher-income persons. Examples include campaign contributions, transportation, subscriptions to sources of political information, payoffs, hiring baby sitters, and the like. Although other costs of participation are not so directly related to socioeconomic classes, costs of information, of obtaining requisite skills, and of the transactions necessary to mobilize members of similar interests and values are probably lower for higher status individuals. Such costs are relatively fixed, and higher SES citizens have usually invested in them for social or economic reasons. Related to these are the lower costs of organizing for political participation to members of groups that have institutionalized mechanisms for mobilizing and informing their membership. For example, members of state real estate organizations receive publications containing information about the times and places of land use hearings, potential courses of action, and political resources available to them. In addition, the higher an individual's SES, the greater the probability that he, as part of his daily activities, reads newspapers, watches local and national news, and discusses politics with friends and neighbors (Doubleday, Godwin, and Orange 1976). All of these activities may be undertaken for reasons unrelated to politics, but they provide spillovers—external benefits—which, in effect, lower the cost of information needed to participate.

The cost of time for participation is more difficult to assess. Presumably it costs the unemployed, the retired, or the nonworking spouse less than persons working for pay to spend time in participatory activity. Among those who must take time from work, persons with higher wages have higher opportunity costs. These costs are difficult to estimate, however, since many workers are released specifically for participation. Salaried individuals—as opposed to employees on wages—may not be docked for time spent in participation. In such cases, the costs are determined by the opportunity costs of activities foregone and whether there would have been deductions if the time were spent in something other than participation.

As an example of how the different components of the expected utility of participation vary with the political activity, we can compare voting with attending a community hearing on a regional land use plan. Riker and Ordeshook (1968) and studies of voting that have followed their model found that D, the pleasure or displeasure derived from the act of participating, accounts for well over half the explained variation between voting and not voting. In stark contrast, when this same model used to predict attendance at a land use hearing (Doubleday et al. 1976), PB could explain 68% of the variance between participants and nonparticipants while D and C could explain less than 5%. When the effects of P and B were separated, the effects of B were by far the more important.

Of all the variables predicting the subjective expected utility of participation, the absolute value of the differential utility between policy options (B) is the most important for the present discussion. The perceived probability of affecting the outcome (P), the utility derived from participation as an activity (D), and the cost of participation (C) all help to explain the favored position enjoyed by higher-status individuals in the American political system, but even within the higher SES stratum only a small portion of the citizenry participates on any given issue, and *the participants vary depending on the perceived importance of the issue to them.* Some groups or individuals participate in educational issues, others in the debate over urban renewal, and still others in the selection of political party leaders (Dahl 1961).

To understand the politics of land use policies it is essential to identify the groups for which an issue is most important because the members of these groups or their representatives are most likely to pay the costs of participation and bring their resources to bear on the decisions. For other citizens, interest in the "correctness" of land use policies may be limited largely to wanting assurance that the policies were determined by legitimate means.

THE IMPORTANCE TO THE DECISION PROCESS OF THE CITIZEN'S ACCESS

To be successful a public policy to control land use must: (1) establish decision-making authority in designated institutions, (2) distribute authority among levels of government, and (3) specify the initial procedures for formulating, adopting, and modifying plans. Each of these actions is procedural or "constitutional"—i.e., they set rules that must be followed when substantive decisions (those which actually determine which land can be used for what purpose) are made. Procedural policies generally precede substantive decisions. In fact, an analysis of four nascent state-level land use policies reported that the current policies consist almost entirely of procedural stipulations (Godwin and Shepard 1975).

When the decisions concerning procedural rules are made in states taking the first steps toward land use policies, questions concerning public access relate to two basic issues. First, how much access should professional planners have vis-à-vis citizens. In resolving this issue states tend to limit the formal access of planners and emphasize citizen involvement in all phases of the process. The second issue is the determination of state and local roles in the development and implementation of land use plans. The ability of different individuals and organizations to participate effectively in the political process depends upon the level of government responsible for a decision. Some groups are better organized for access at the state level while others are more effective with city or county governments. For example, local developers, savings and loan associations, and neighborhood groups have much better access at the city or county level, but large regional developers, national or state environmental groups, and state bureaucracies such as the state housing office are organized for participation and influence at the state level. States currently tend to emphasize the local role in the development and implementation of land use plans. This tendency is, in part, an expression of the widely held belief that local rather than state-level planning will be most responsive to citizens' demands. In both of these issues government officials, whether appointed or elected, emphasize the importance of citizen involvement in and public access to the decision process.

The need to determine the public's preference for land use policies is the ostensible purpose for encouraging citizen involvement and access. However, public access has several other roles, including legitimating government actions, securing political quiescence from a large majority of citizens, and politically socializing citizens.

Determining Public Preferences

Because of the economic and political costs of correcting mistakes—relocating public facilities or reconverting land from residential to agricultural use—accurate planning—coupled with control—is a highly valued good. Since accurate information concerning public preferences would presumably reduce the incidence of such changes, elections, hearings, workshops, citizen advisory committees, and surveys have all been used to obtain such information.

If land use policies are to provide public goods and services at levels approaching the social optimum, then political participation must be representative.[4] However, as indicated above, only a small percentage of citizens will participate in land use decisions, and they are not representative of the general public. *Because of the inequalities of political influence, however, from the point of view of the political decision-maker, the preferences of a representative sample of citizens are of little value. Rather, the political decision-maker wishes to know the opinions of those who are likely to demand access to future land use decisions.* These persons will be most important in supporting the decision-maker, the institutions established for making future land use decisions, and the future decisions. The best available predictor of which groups are likely to demand future access is current participation. Thus, "biased samples" of preferences are particularly valuable to decision-makers.

The need to obtain "unrepresentative" preferences does not occur because decision-makers are evil or undemocratic; on the contrary, to the extent that decision-makers are required to be responsive, they are required to be so by the politically active. Regardless of the reasons for responding to an unrepresentative sample of public opinion, such responses facilitate the maintenance of support for land use decisions and the decision process.

Determining the Salience of Public Preferences

For decision-makers, information on people's preferences is insufficient; information on the salience of preferences is also needed to allow decision-makers to identify the compromises which will maintain political support. To know only that a minority prefer preserving a

4. Needless to say, "the social optimum" has not and probably cannot be empirically determined for any particular public good or public service or any mix of them. Certain public goods, such as freedom of speech or religion, are in a totally different category from air quality or esthetic views. For the public goods and services relevant to this study, however, if certain assumptions about values and about the distribution of public preferences are made, a social optimum theoretically can be specified. If we assume that for the types of public goods and services relevant here, the "optimal" level of a public good or service is at or near the point where any other level would increase the level of dissatisfaction of the citizenry and if we assume that the preference curve for each good or service is normal, then a public good will be supplied at the level desired by that individual whose personal utility for the good is at the median (Buchanan and Tullock 1962). Similarly, in the provision of public services the quantity of the service will be at the level desired by the consumer with the median income (Bergstrom and Goodman 1973). These social optima can be achieved only if the political influence of all citizens is equal and decision-makers respond to citizen influence. Such a definition of optimum assumes a number of conditions such as single peaked preference curves and equal information costs (see Black 1968, Breton 1974, Godwin and Shepard 1976). With (or perhaps in spite of) all these assumptions, the basic common sense expectation is fulfilled: unequal levels of political influence will lead to suboptimal distribution of goods and rights by the public sector.

particular "open space" while a majority prefer development is not particularly useful information. The minority may be vehement in its position and seek to punish the decision-maker if the open space is not preserved while the majority may care little about the issue and decide whether or not to support the decision-maker on the basis of other issues more important to them. Making participation costly provides the information on significance needed to maintain political support: people are more likely to pay the costs of participation as the importance .of the issue (B in the equation given above) increases.

Knowing the salience of preferences may be useful for reasons other than maintaining political support. Information on salience may promote an allocation of resources among public goods which is efficient in the sense of maximizing the utility individuals receive from the mix provided. In the private market, one tends to assume that resources will be allocated efficiently among private goods because demand is a function of the relationship between price and quantity. For public goods and services, it is more difficult to get people to reveal their true preferences. Schemes can be imagined such as vote selling (Tullock 1970) or zoning auctions (Clawson 1971, pp. 184–186). At present, political systems have mechanisms for helping to assess the worth of a particular quantity of a public good to an individual or group. Legislative vote trading (the representative from one district votes for a project in another district in return for similar support) is the classic example and occurs at all levels of government.[5] The imposition of participation costs through mechanisms to limit public access is another. Crude as these mechanisms may be (for example, putting notices of hearings in fine print on the classified ads pages, holding a public hearing during working hours, or allowing a meeting to go from 7 P.M. to 3 A.M.), the willingness of an individual or group to cope with them is a measure of the value of a particular decision to the individual or group. Again, mechanisms imperfect from an egalitarian perspective serve important purposes from the perspective of the decision-maker.

Legitimacy
Political legitimacy is a characteristic of the policies and policy-making procedures that people accept because they conform to their

---

5. Legislative vote trading, sometimes called "logrolling," permits people to exchange their support on an issue they do not feel strongly about for the support of others on another issue that has higher utility to them. If votes could be traded for dollars, then participants in voluntary transactions would presumably believe that the transaction has made them better off. Since votes cannot be sold for dollars, logrolling permits votes on one issue to be "sold" for votes on another issue.

values (Friedrich 1963). Maintaining perceptions of political legitimacy is important to both decision-makers and citizens and thus becomes an item of social value in and of itself. Legitimacy is, in a sense, the glue that holds together a functioning political system made up of citizens with conflicting interests. Political legitimacy maintains the popular support necessary for a political system to act upon various demands. In addition, legitimacy reduces compliance costs. When citizens voluntarily behave in accordance with policies because they accept them as legitimate, fewer resources need be allocated to compliance.

Although a particular policy may not conform to an individual's values, he may consider it legitimate if he accepts the legitimacy of the process that produced it. *Political legitimacy can often be transferred from a policy-making process to a particular policy.* In fact, procedures rather than actual decisions appear to be the origin of most people's perception of political legitimacy. Thus, it is not surprising to find that when land use legislation is under consideration, a preponderance of legislative attention is directed toward the detailed design and specification of procedures.

To be legitimate, procedures must conform to people's values. In some countries the relevant values might be labeled "nationalism," "Marxism," "Maoism," or "anticolonialism." In the United States, an important value is "popular consent" or—to be more accurate—the *possibility* of popular participation and veto. Providing mechanisms for public access thus contributes to legitimation. Note that it is the *provision* of such mechanisms—not necessarily their effectiveness or representativeness—that contributes to the legitimacy of the policies. The presence or absence of such mechanisms can be, and usually is, made quite visible, but the ultimate effectiveness and representativeness are much more difficult for the citizen to ascertain.

When the opportunity for public access is provided, citizens are almost forced to accord legitimacy to the resulting decisions. Around election time newspaper editors are fond of reminding people that if they do not vote they cannot complain about the result. This is a corollary: if you vote, you cannot complain either. By participating, you support—that is you recognize as legitimate—the procedures by which decisions are made. To illustrate how legitimacy is transferred from decision process to decision outcome, assume you are in a group that is deciding where they will eat dinner. The members of the group, including you, agree to abide by the decision of the majority. A vote is taken and your preference loses, but you accept the decision and its legitimacy because you accepted the decision process and had the opportunity to participate in it. To the extent that there is a transfer of legitimacy from process to final decisions, decisions will be accorded legitimacy by the citizenry.

Often the use of elected representatives—establishing procedural legitimacy through elections—is sufficient to assure the legitimacy of the policies decided upon by those representatives. Where decisions are anticipated that do not conform to the strongly held values of many people, additional trappings may be required to strengthen perceptions of legitimacy. This has been the case with land use. Because decision-makers have anticipated the strongly held values of people concerning their rights in real property and the rights of the state vis-à-vis their property, land use legislation invokes requirements such as sequences of hearings, timely notice, and citizen committees—public access mechanisms to increase perceptions of legitimacy. As long as this perception is created, land use control is more likely to be seen as legitimate, even by losers. From the perspective of the political system, observations that "timely notices" are buried in the classified section or that citizen advisory committees are not representative are irrelevant so long as legitimacy is fostered. In the words of one unusually percep-tive and open (and former) director of a state land use agency, public hearings are held "to defuse public opinion."

Political Quiescence

Closely related to the role of public access in legitimating both the decision process and the decisions themselves is the role of promised public access in reducing demands by the public for material alloca-tions. This reduction in demands, known as obtaining political quies-cence (Edelman 1976), allows political leaders to allocate scarce re-sources to the groups and individuals that have the organization and influence to reward or punish the political decision-makers. The reduc-tion of demands also keeps the political system from becoming "over-loaded" to the point where the decision-making process is immobilized.

When changes are made at the constitutional level, the prospect of these changes and uncertainty over their outcome may create a high level of anxiety throughout society (Edelman 1971). In these situa-tions, most individuals do not have fixed opinions concerning the de-sirability of one set of rules over another. Instead, their positions are highly malleable, and government activities are a major, if not *the* major, factor in shaping public opinion. In these situations government can create opinions about what is proper and form expectations about what should come. Thus, government can satisfy many people not by meeting their substantive demands but by changing those demands.

Land use planning, particularly at its present stage, where

constitutional-level changes are being advocated, is an excellent example of this type of situation. A statewide opinion survey in 1970 indicated that 70% of Oregon's adult population opposed land use planning (Harris 1970). By 1973, however, a similar poll showed 70% of the state's registered voters favored land use planning at the state level (Yaden and Associates, Inc. 1973).[6] It can be reasonably assumed that this dramatic change was influenced by the vigorous support of land use by the governor and the tremendous publicity given to the public hearings held all over the state by the Oregon Land Conservation and Development Commission (LCDC).

Public support for state land use planning was produced not by giving the public any tangible resources—the legislation allocating such resources was still several years away—but by providing them with symbolic goods (perhaps they might be called "psychic goods"). Symbolic goods give their recipients feelings of status, identity, and security (Mitchell and Mitchell 1969). For example, the LCDC assured the public that it would further the goals of economic development, conservation, and the preservation of agricultural land. In addition, public access at the local level was provided through public hearings that gave all citizens the right to make inputs into the decision process, and guarantees of appeal procedures to the courts were made. Through its manipulation of valued symbols such as "development," "conservation," "preservation," "the right to access," "local-level decision-making," and "the provision of appeals procedures," the LCDC provided status and security. Whether you favored development, conservation, or preservation you were assured your interests would be protected and the decision process would be fair.

Neither the seeming incompatibility between the goals of "conservation" and "development" nor the fact that the ability to contact members of the LCDC to present information is concentrated in well-organized groups is likely to threaten the perception of the general public that they and the land are protected by the commission (Doubleday et al. 1976). Instead, the unorganized general public is likely to be satisfied by the symbolic goods and remain quiescent and unorganized, thereby allowing the regulatory agency to spend its tangible resources satisfying the demands of the organized groups whose interests are immediately and specifically affected by land use decisions (Edelman 1971, pp. 21–23).

6. Although the polls were carried out by two different organizations, the wording of the questions and their placement among other related questions was held as constant as possible since the sponsor of the second poll was interested in the specific issue of whether or not a change in opinion had occurred.

Political Socialization

In the above discussion of the importance of public access to political decision-makers and to the political system itself, most of the emphasis concerns the desirability of giving the image (symbol) of access while, in fact, making participation sufficiently difficult to discourage all but the most interested citizens. Wider participation can, however, be useful to the political system *in the long run*. As early as 1860 John Stuart Mill, in his *Considerations on Representative Government,* noted that widespread participation is not necessary to produce the best decisions today but to produce better citizens tomorrow. Mill believed, and contemporary studies on political socialization and participation support him (Lipset 1960, Chaps, 4, 12, Cole 1933, Kramer 1972), that political participation helped educate persons to be more tolerant, broaden their horizons, and make them more effective in other aspects of their lives. In this way participation could improve the adaptability of the political system and allow greater diversity of ideas without violence and prejudice. Although it is often presumed that most political socialization occurs when citizens are children (Easton and Dennis 1969, Jaros 1973), public access and political participation may still have the important educational effects on adults suggested by Mill.

REGULATION

Implicit in our discussion of land use control criteria, public participation, and the role of public access is the high degree of tension between the accomplishment of certain objectives considered desirable in the development of land use plans and the feasibility of obtaining the requisite levels of participation. This tension is not unique to land use regulation. An examination of many studies of regulatory policies by Edelman (1971) led him to the following generalizations:

1. Material goods—e.g., money, land, and perhaps power—are given to organized groups in proportion to their relative bargaining strength.
2. Symbolic goods reassure the unorganized that their appeals are noted and something is being done, and the unorganized remain unorganized and quiescent.
3. Conflict is ritualized and regularized in regulatory agencies to reduce anxiety and uncertainty and to legitimate authority.
4. Organized groups use political agencies to make good their claims on tangible resources.

From our analysis of political participation it is not difficult to understand why these four patterns develop whether the substantive area of regulation is interstate commerce, public utilities, or land use control. Regulations must first determine procedural rules concerning how, when, and by whom the final allocations of material goods will be made. The long-term importance and complexity of procedural rules and their determination are typically understood only by those already familiar with both the substantive issues and the workings of government institutions. For example, a local developer or a lobbyist for the Sierra Club is likely to understand the probable effects on him of a decision to allocate land use control to the state rather than the county. Similarly, attorneys specializing in real property, planners, local developers, permanently organized political action groups, and other individuals who deal frequently with property decisions can estimate the costs and benefits to them of procedural decisions concerning who can bring suit, what types of appeals are available, how and by whom compensation will be decided, and at what point in the decision process citizen participation is required. Those unfamiliar with the procedural process—and that includes most citizens—will probably neither understand the relevance of these decisions to them nor attempt to participate in structuring the decision process.

The following analogy illustrates the importance of procedural rules. If you and someone whose values are quite opposed to your own had, between you, the opportunity to select the next president of the United States, and the procedural rules were that one of you nominate ten persons and the other select the president from the nominees, would you prefer to choose the original ten or choose one from among them? Most of us would prefer to select the original pool of ten persons since we could presumably find at least ten persons whose values were similar to our own. In many respects setting procedural rules is like selecting the initial ten; these rules limit the conflict and reduce the alternatives so that the final allocations by the political system are like choosing one from among ten. Although the excitement and publicity may center around the second decision, the scope of that decision has been so limited by the first choice that it is far less important.

Because setting up procedures seems far removed from making final allocations and because of the complexity of procedural rules, only a few people can accurately estimate the benefits and costs of participating in this process. A young person just moving into a state who expects to save for several years before making the down payment on a house is not likely to become involved in setting up procedures for land use decisions even though these procedures will significantly affect the availability, price, and quality of the housing he will ultimately choose.

Regulatory Agencies

In the development of complex procedural rules, the time and information costs required to reach decisions on these rules quite often encourage legislatures to set up regulatory agencies to develop and implement these rules. When there is little conflict among the regulated, they are often allowed to regulate themselves. For example, the rules for licensing doctors are usually developed and administered by state boards of medical examiners composed of M.D.s. When there is conflict, however, the regulatory agencies are generally composed of representatives from each of the major interests. For example, the Interstate Commerce Commission may be composed of an ex-railroad official, an ex-trucking president, and ex-airline executive, and perhaps a labor representative. Similarly, in Oregon the Land Conservation and Development Commission is composed of a realtor, an attorney active in environmental organizations, a farmer, a marine biologist, a local government official, a former director of the state's Department of Environmental Quality, and a past president of the League of Women Voters. Through such a membership, major organized interests are represented.

Defenders of this system of representation suggest that the pluralistic membership of the agency helps insure that there are countervailing powers and that no single elite will dominate the political process, thereby protecting the public (see, for example, Dahl 1961, Polsby 1963). Critics suggest that rather than protecting the public, such a system only protects the organized from each other while allowing them to exploit the unorganized (see, for example, Bachrach and Baratz 1970, Wolff 1965, Lowi 1969). In land use politics an analysis of four states with land use planning agencies tends to support the latter view (Godwin and Shepard 1975).

Altering the Pattern of Regulatory Agency Capture by the Regulated

Regulatory agencies are captured by the regulated, in part, because legislatures delegate broad discretion to agencies without establishing clear standards to be used in deciding issues. Often, as is the case with land use policy in Oregon, the regulatory agency itself is charged with the task of developing standards. Critics of the resultant interest-group politics in the administration of policy argue for a "juridical democracy" in which standards are decided in the legislative phase where, it is assumed, visibility is higher and participation broader (Lowi 1969). However, so long as the political quiescence of unorganized citizens can be maintained through symbolic outputs, juridical democracy is unlikely.

Symbolic outputs do not always result in political quiescence. Although *Brown vs. Board of Education of Topeka* (1954) was largely symbolic, involving the three elements of identity, status, and morality, it did facilitate further efforts for school desegregation. A key element in this situation was the organization of blacks into politically powerful voting and lobbying groups. Rather than encouraging quiescence, the decision became a useful tool in further organizational efforts.

Exceptions to the rule that the organized get tangible resources and the unorganized get symbolic goods appear to share three characteristics. First, the unorganized who receive the symbolic goods of status and identity use them to facilitate organization. Second, the receivers of the symbolic good move to a different political arena where the symbol is more powerful than the bargaining leverage of the organized groups. (For example, blacks moved from attempting to achieve desegregation or voting rights at the local level and obtained new legislation and enforcement from Washington.) Finally, for recipients of the symbolic goods, the material problem remained. In most issues involving regulation it is far more difficult to determine whether or not a policy has achieved its goals, since the goals are broader and more difficult to evaluate than is the case with overt discrimination.

The tactic of changing the location of a decision could be important in land use regulation because two of the major groups which have limited the effectiveness of zoning at the local level may be less effective at the state level. The cost of zoning changes has often been acceptable to local developers when compared to their benefits. Such changes could be both more costly and less probable at the state level.[7] Similarly, the costs to a neighborhood group organizing to prevent the development of multiple-family or higher-use activities in their neighborhood are higher when the decision is made at the state level.

The regulated also influence regulatory agencies because they control the information and expertise required by the agencies. While they may have no conspiratorial motives, the ability of the regulated to provide information that would otherwise be costly to an agency gains

---

7. Note that the statement applies only to local developers. Large developers tend to support centralized, state-level, land use control over decentralized control. A large developer with, perhaps, one central office supervising operations in several states can be influential at the state level while there would be much larger total costs if he had to participate in decisions made in numerous localities. The large developer may also anticipate a political disadvantage if he has to compete at the local level with local developers.

them attention and access. As will be shown in the following chapters, specific land use control mechanisms require extensive information. The equity and efficiency of such techniques as TDRs will be affected by the sources of information used to determine land value or to estimate the nature of the demand for development rights. Reduction in the influence of the regulated would require that schemes such as TDRs be accompanied with appropriations to pay the full costs of the information they require for implementation. The role of a national land use bill subsidizing this information-gathering process might be exceptionally important in this regard.

The influence of the regulated over regulatory agencies is only one manifestation of an encompassing pattern of politics in America. American institutions are designed to be responsive to individual and group demands at all stages of the political process, but such institutions designed to be responsive to numerous constituencies are not well equipped to articulate and implement, integrated, coherent policy programs. For example, although a legislator must pay attention to the interests of active constituents, the party's platform can usually be ignored with little likelihood of reprisal. The result of responsiveness to multiple constituencies is the lack of any institution that can be held responsible for developing and instituting programmatic policies for the entire society.

Some argue that the solution to this problem lies in ideological politics. While there is little chance of quickly altering so fundamental a pattern, one can analyze land use policy-making proposals in terms of resolving or compounding the problems associated with existing political patterns. Some argue that the solution to unrepresentative land use control is even greater citizen involvement at all stages of policy development; but, as pointed out earlier, goals committees, citizen advisory boards, and endless public hearings only compound the advantages of certain groups. Such procedures usually emphasize reaching consensus early in policy making. The result is usually a laundry list of objectives important to the most easily activated participants but no attempt to decide areas of conflict among the participants. Because of the laundry-list approach, the door is left open to responsive, but possibly irresponsible, policy implementation and administration. This is the classic case of regulatory politics where the resolution of conflict is ad hoc, on a case by case basis, and only the organized, most directly affected parties are likely to participate. Only when groups are willing to participate regularly, day after day and year after year, will the regulatory agency respond.[8]

8. Galanter (1974) discusses this pattern with respect to the legal system. He notes

The disorganization of already organized groups is a factor which could make land use planning less symbolic and perhaps more responsive to the material interests of current nonparticipants. In effect, participation costs for current participants could be raised by disrupting organizational advantages or by altering the usefulness of existing interest group organizations. The former tactic when it has been previously attempted has not been very successful, e.g., the Sherman Anti-Trust Act. This tactic would seem amenable to planning mechanisms that rely on "the market" such as TDRs and marginal cost pricing of public services related to distance and settlement patterns. Of course, to the extent that such planning mechanisms would alter the influence which organized groups currently have, these groups will oppose the introduction of the policies and stop the control before it is started.

POLITICAL ACCEPTABILITY

Understanding what influences the political acceptability of particular techniques of land use control can be useful to persons investigating new techniques in three ways. First, knowledge of the probable acceptability of policy alternatives can help to direct their efforts toward techniques that have at least some chance of being implemented and thus better channel their time and effort. Second, analysts proposing new techniques should know how the specifics of these policies are likely to be changed by the political system. For example, a policy designed to capture windfalls will rely on some mechanism for measuring windfalls, or, given the ability of participants to shift costs to nonparticipants, those suggesting a policy change might wish to examine how likely this might be for each alternative and how it could be prevented. The third, and closely related, reason for examining political acceptability is to uncover unanticipated consequences of policy proposals. The "wars" on poverty, crime, and Vietnam all had significant unanticipated and undesirable consequences. A war on the inefficiencies and inequities in land use will also generate unintended effects. It is to be hoped that a better understanding of the differences between the ways participants (including public officials) in the political arena and the ways outside analysts calculate benefits and costs will alert outside analysts to the pitfalls that may be ahead.

Although a better understanding of political acceptability is useful, speculations concerning the political feasibility of any policy are sub-

its application to the regulatory process as well by citing a women's movement lobbyist who stated: "By coming back week after week . . . we tell them not only that we are here, but that we are here to stay. We're not here to scare anybody. . . . The most threatening thing I can say is that we'll be back" (*New York Times* Jan. 29, 1974, p. 34).

ject to significant error. Our knowledge of political acceptability consists largely of broad generalities, and each policy in each situation has some unique characteristics. Also important as a limitation on the accuracy of political predictions is the seemingly endless number of variations shown by techniques such as ZED or TDR when one moves from the conceptual level to actual specification of how the technique will be implemented and administered.

Given these limitations, what general factors affecting political acceptability can be reliably identified? We suggest three dimensions that may be particularly useful: (1) changes from the status quo in the values considered and the participants involved in land use planning, (2) the certainty of the outcome, and (3) the clarity with which beneficiaries can identify the political source of their benefits and the losers the source of their new costs.

Changing Values and Participants

Current land use control policies—or the lack thereof—did not arise from happenstance. They persist because they serve the interests of politically active citizens. Local zoning ordinances, building codes, subdivision controls, and statutes on annexation and municipal incorporation have apparently served certain values and interests of citizens of above average SES well. The "quality" of their neighborhoods has been protected from invasion by undesirable citizens, land uses, and low-cost or multiple-dwelling units. Property values have not only been protected but have risen. Variance procedures have been sufficiently responsive to block undesired developments in their neighborhoods but permit higher SES citizens to profit from speculation and development.

To conclude that something more than cosmetic alterations in the status quo is feasible requires one or more of several suppositions. One might reason that innovations in social technology, e.g., TDRs, will demonstrate that established interests in land use policy can be served better. Or one might suppose that either the interests people seek through land use policy or the relative responsiveness of the political system to citizens with different interests have been or can be changed. The first possibility is considered below in the section on certainty of outcomes, the latter is the subject of this section.

Certainly the hoopla surrounding the adoption of state land use acts suggests that land use policy will serve such new values as environmental protection and energy conservation. Many social scientists who have studied the impetus toward the provision of environmental preservation, open space, and the "steady state" have suggested that these are luxury goods (Edel 1973, p. 109, Trop and Roos 1971, p. 59, Harry et al. 1969). Those who support these values tend to be persons who have reached a position where decreasing marginal returns on the consumption of food, clothing, shelter, and consumer durables leads them to allocate increasing portions of their income toward the preservation of the environment. The entrance of these values and associated interests into the politics of land use changes both the social efficiency and the political acceptability of different land use controls. If environmental goods are becoming more valued and goods associated with growth less valued as median income increases, then the costs and benefits assigned to different land use objectives will change, and there will be a different optimal efficiency outcome. The political acceptability of different land use controls may also change since support for such objectives as environmental protection, open space, and the restriction of growth will be strongest among citizens who, because of their higher socioeconomic status, have higher rates of political participation.[9] This support can be expected to increase to the extent that average income rises and allows the purchase of these "luxury goods" (Rattan 1971). The combination of these tendencies provides a basis for asserting that a change in or addition to the interests politically active citizens seek through land use policies has occurred. And, to the extent that interests have been changed, alternative land use control techniques to serve the new interests may be feasible. Thus, the feasibility of particular techniques of land use control can be partially estimated by identifying the new interests and considering the degree to which these techniques serve them better than techniques now in use.

However, such analysis should not ignore the possibility that the interests currently served by land use policies have not diminished in their importance to politically active citizens. Citizen interests in neighborhood quality, increasing property values, and profits from modest speculation in land are likely to remain strong and are, perhaps, still the highest priority interests sought through government land use control policies. Moreover, repeated studies show no change in a widespread preference for a residential style characterized by single-family homes on quarter-acre lots in settings more rural than urban within 30 to 45 minutes driving time from a metropolitan center. In assessing the political feasibility of an alternative technique one must consider not only new interests but also current, strongly held interests. Since new interests (e.g., conservation) may conflict

9. It should not be assumed that because most support for environmental issues comes from persons with higher incomes most higher income persons support these values or that support for these issues is great. As the recession and oil shortage indicated, persons may rapidly revise their support for ecology or opposition to growth if they suffer such negative effects as reduced employment security.

with old interests (e.g., profits from development) an analysis of the political acceptability of a land control technique must include the relative values politically active citizens attach to conflicting preferences and the preferences that will be enhanced by the technique.

We suggest, at the risk of oversimplification, that three major groups of citizens participate in land use policy formation: (1) individuals who profit from increased development, including builders, savings and loan institutions, local retail establishments, and realtors; (2) individuals who organize at the neighborhood level on an ad hoc basis to contest a pending decision; and (3) individuals who highly value alleviation of the damage to the environment often associated with development.[10] The political acceptability of alternative techniques for land use control will depend on how well the techniques suit the demands of all active participants. The demands of the three groups are neither entirely discordant nor entirely compatible. For example, neighborhood interest groups may ally themselves with development groups in opposition to environmentalists on the issue of centralized versus decentralized land use control. Environmentalists may get support from neighborhood groups when they advocate control techniques to limit development, protect the stability and quality of local communities from the influx of "outsiders," and increase property values by restricting the supply of residential land. One must consider, therefore, the compromises among the three groups that might be fostered by alternative land use control techniques. To analyze fully the probability that a policy will be chosen, one must consider how techniques could be designed and packaged so as to meet some demands of the less organized or influential groups through symbolic reassurances yet guarantee material distribution to the best organized and most influential groups. If the technique is implemented at the state level, neighborhood interests are the most obvious candidates to receive symbolic assurances rather than material goods.

The emergence of environmental groups has increased the feasibility of an expanded state role in land use planning. Although it was once possible to meet the demands of environmentalists with symbolic assurances, they have come to exert increasing influence, slowing the

10. The discussion of these three groups, their interests, objectives, and sources of interest are developed more fully elsewhere (Godwin and Shepard 1975). A fourth group, the farm interests, is not included in this discussion since they do not have a unified position. Agricultural landowners farthest from the urban fringe tend to side with the environmentalists to "preserve prime agricultural lands" through tax incentives. Those near or at the fringe tend to side with development interests so as to maintain their option to convert their lands from agricultural to residential or commercial use. Both groups tend to lobby, when possible, for a combination of both benefits: tax reductions with the option to convert at a later date.

rate and increasing the cost of development by challenging environmental impact statements, securing court injunctions, and using other judicial procedures. A technique acceptable to both environmentalists and developers would probably include such items as paying for preservation with public funds, allowing development in specified areas, and limiting the judicial recourse of groups challenging such development. This would reduce the ability of neighborhood groups to stop development and place the cost of preservation on the general public.

Considerations of political feasibility are not completed by matching probable participants and alternative policies. Implementing the very policies thus made feasible may further alter participation. For example, there are indications in Vermont and Oregon that an expanded state role in land use control—whether active or largely made up of symbolic reassurances to neighborhood groups and environmentalists—has nevertheless provoked participation by citizens who perceive and value deeply a connection between property and liberty. Stated differently, one should not attempt an analysis of political acceptability with a model of the political process that does not allow values, political self-interest, and participation to interact. Participation and the interests articulated are functions of what becomes politically and socially accepted.

Certainty of Outcomes

Certainty of outcome is valued by most persons, particularly by the politically influential. Policies exist, for the most part, because they benefit politically influential citizens who have little incentive to risk existing benefits unless increased benefits are probable or current benefits are likely to change. Because of the value of certainty, policy usually develops incrementally: "new" policies are only marginal changes from previous policies. Such slight deviations from the known and familiar also reduce information costs, and, for this reason incremental decision-making is defended as a reasonable way to make policy (Lindblom 1959, see also Etzioni 1967). Reasonable or not, incrementalism is likely to be unavoidable because it assures politically influential participants of two major benefits: (1) they find incremental changes less dangerous to their interests, and (2) they get feedback on the effects of any changes before proceeding further.

Some land use control techniques are advocated not as a response to new interests but as innovations in social technology that permit more efficient responses to existing situations. The political acceptability of such alternatives depends heavily on how certain the promised "efficiencies" appear to be. Certainty, and hence political acceptability, are related to several factors. In general, the more a proposed policy deviates from existing policies, the less certain are its outcomes. When major deviations from existing policies are proposed, certainty can be improved by vesting the regulation, implementation, and adjustment of the new policy in the most organized, influential participants, a practice typical of regulatory policies. For example, the rules for regulating and licensing physicians, attorneys, and realtors were largely drawn up by the groups involved. Again using an example from Oregon, the state land use bill could not get out of committee until the chairman turned it over to its major opponents and allowed them to add new goals and objectives as well as set the initial procedural rules for implementing state controls (speech by L. B. Day, director, LCDC, April 1976).

A second technique for making proposed policies more acceptable is to remove a large portion of their potential negative effects if the promised gains in efficiency are not realized or are distributed in a manner unacceptable to the active participants. This could be accomplished by including procedures that generously compensate the politically influential if they experience losses. This tactic might be particularly useful in dealing with a technique like TDRs which requires a period of operation to generate the feedback needed to "fine tune" the control technique. Such compensation would not be a permanent aspect of the technique but would be included for an initial period, after which the TDR market would be governed as prescribed by its advocates without the necessity for additional compensation.

Identifying the Benefactor

If the political decision-maker judges policies by their effect on his own political position, he will be motivated to allocate benefits to a group only if they can clearly identify him as the source of the largess. Thus, the political acceptability of land use control techniques will depend upon the clarity with which advantaged groups can identify (and hence reward) their benefactors. There is, of course, a corollary: political feasibility is enhanced for some techniques when those who bear the costs have difficulty in identifying the misanthrope.

Marginal cost pricing is a land use control technique which illustrates the applicability of the identity criterion. Its benefits are diffuse among citizens and accrue over long periods of time. Citizens who benefit are likely to perceive neither the benefit nor the benefactor, but the costs, and their source, will be more obvious to the citizens who suddenly must pay for services at higher rates. For this reason, the technique is not likely to receive support from either participants or decision-makers.

The criterion of identity has an additional implication applicable to estimating the feasibility of land use control techniques that propose "windfall" recapture and/or "wipeout" compensation. For these techniques, political feasibility will depend upon the clarity of the windfall, the clarity of the wipeout, and the clarity of the windfall recapture. Techniques that provide compensation for wipeouts without recapturing windfalls will, in general, be preferred to those that provide wipeout compensation through windfall recapture. This generalization depends upon the relationship between the magnitude of clear compensation required and the availability of revenues from persons who cannot clearly identify their losses.

SUMMARY

Although the politician may be interested in efficiency issues, he must deal mainly with questions related to distribution. We have suggested throughout this chapter that political decision-makers and political participants act rationally to insure that their benefits from any policy outweigh their costs. Because upper SES citizens have distinct resource and organizational advantages, they participate more frequently and more effectively. So long as those who govern are held responsible to the governed through citizen participation, political decision-makers and participants will seek advantages through the system by disadvantaging nonparticipants. We have suggested that because politics focuses on distribution issues, reducing external costs, moving toward the optimal in the provision of public goods, reducing the total cost of public services, and citing other efficiency arguments will not strongly interest politicians or politically active citizens because both groups receive the advantages of "inefficient" land use controls.

This argument does not mean that economists should stop examining efficiency problems or that citizen participation should be curtailed and planning left to a "benevolent" planner. Rather, the discussion suggests that existing institutional incentives for inefficiency and inequity must be considered when land use control techniques are examined and proposed. Achieving the desired efficiencies will probably entail accepting short-run inefficiencies while institutionalizing the more efficient techniques. In the political arena both politicians and participants can change rapidly, and, for this reason, future benefits tend to be heavily discounted compared with current benefits. Understanding this allows those suggesting new techniques for improving efficiency to make their proposals more acceptable by increasing the short-term certainty of benefits to politically influential groups.

Just as efficiency need not be dropped as an acceptable goal, current inequities in participation need not be interpreted as a rationale for reducing participation. Rather, land use control techniques might seek mechanisms to equalize overall participation without diminishing it. As discussed above, the benefits of participation include not only information about citizen preference but also political legitimacy and the socialization to greater citizen responsibility.

✳️ *Chapter 5*

Zoning

Zoning has been the most influential public technique for controlling private land use in America during the twentieth century. Quite simply, zoning is the practice of dividing a land area such as a city or county into districts within which only specified activities may take place. The traditional rationale for zoning has been the elimination of the "undesirable" external effects that characterize "uncontrolled" urban land use. A list of these external effects would include air and water pollution, excessive noise levels, traffic congestion, and esthetic disamenities. Because of its predominant role, zoning is now being proposed to encompass expanded objectives for supplying certain public goods such as the preservation of open space, prime agricultural land, and critical environmental areas. But before advocating this expanded role, we should review zoning's past performance in eliminating external effects and attempt to project its potential for providing public goods.

For readers unfamiliar with zoning the initial part of this chapter provides a brief overview of the structure and history of American zoning regulations. The second section establishes a framework for evaluating some of the major benefits and costs of employing zoning for land use control. Each of the individual benefits and costs is then treated, and the question of who benefits from zoning and pays for it is addressed next. Finally, some aspects of the political acceptability of expanding the role of zoning are explored.

BACKGROUND

As used here, *zoning* will specify municipal zoning, where municipal refers to any political subdivision of a state, i.e., city, village, town, or county.[1] Other forms of direct regulation in land development such as subdivision regulations or building codes, will not be specifically analyzed although they also are exercises of the police power—the power to protect and promote the health, safety, convenience, and general welfare of a community.

The Structure of Zoning

Functionally, zoning is a means for spatially separating "incompatible" land uses.[2] Preventing a slaughterhouse from being located in a residential neighborhood is a striking example. The mechanics of separation require the designation of specific land use districts to include varying intensities of residential use (single, multiple, or high-density multiple family), different types of commercial activity (neighborhood, limited, highway, or central business district), varying degrees of industrial use (light, medium, or heavy), and other classifications including institutional and agricultural uses. The number of classifications varies among municipalities and usually increases with the size of a municipality and the diversity of its social and economic structure.

Within each land use district, various regulations and restrictions apply to (1) the use of land (permitted uses, lot areas, setback requirements, parking facilities, open space requirements), (2) the height, size, and use of buildings, and (3) the density of population. Zoning ordinances define procedures for allowing exceptions to these restrictions such as variances, conditional uses, and planned unit developments, all of which may be granted by administrative authority. Rules for uses which were "nonconforming" when the ordinance was adopted are also included.

Although most states have adopted similar enabling laws delegating zoning powers to municipalities, a standard set of principles and procedures does not exist. As a consequence, considerable discretion is allowed in the writing of zoning ordinances, and they vary sig-

---

1. This background is drawn primarily from Barlowe (1972, pp. 537–549) and Babcock (1966, pp. 3–18), although there are many other good presentations of the structure and history of zoning. For a more detailed account, see Delafons (1969) or Toll (1969).
2. Those familiar with recent modifications in zoning, e.g., planned unit developments, may take exception to the basic structure described here. However, zoning modifications are still a form of direct regulation based on the police power. For our purposes, little is lost by focusing on the fundamental structure of zoning. For those interested in new legal, administrative, and economic concepts and techniques related to zoning, see Marcus and Groves (1970).

nificantly among municipalities. Depending on your perspective, this has advantages or disadvantages. On the one hand, each municipality is allowed to construct a zoning ordinance to suit its unique social and physical characteristics within the broad guidelines of the enabling legislation. On the other, this discretion may result in disadvantaging particular groups of existing or potential residents. Zoning decisions are, of course, subject to court appeal, but this is often a time consuming and costly process, and unequal treatment is difficult to prove.[3]

The History of Zoning

The evolution of zoning in the twentieth century helps to understand its present structure. Land regulation prior to the twentieth century was sporadic and dealt primarily with safety and nuisances. Banning gunpowder manufacture and storage from populated areas represented a safety measure, and nuisances like tanneries or brick kilns were restricted from residential and business districts. Zoning for land use planning began in Boston from 1904 to 1905 when districts with varying building heights were established and in Los Angeles from 1909 to 1911 when seven industrial districts were separated from residential areas.

The impetus for the first comprehensive zoning ordinance sprang from a 1910 New York Commission on Heights of Buildings which investigated the impact of skyscrapers on community health and safety. The commission's 1913 report recommended regulations controlling the height, bulk, and use of buildings in different districts. What external effect prompted the recommendations? The commission was established in answer to efforts of the Fifth Avenue Association, a merchants' organization concerned with the effect of sidewalk traffic from lower-class workers on business in their exclusive shops. The garment industry, a primary employer of the lower-class workers, was locating in the upper stories of buildings in and below midtown Manhattan, and the merchants were convinced that limitations on building heights would curb or slow the flow of these workers. The first comprehensive zoning ordinance was recommended in 1916 by a subsequent commission. It provided height and bulk controls and setback requirements throughout the city. Commentators questioned the constitutionality of the proposed regulations because it restricted private property rights by public control. Some advocated use of the power of eminent domain with attendant compensation for the restricted private property rights.

3. The recent New Jersey decision in *South Burlington NAACP vs. Mt. Laurel Township (1975)*, is one of the recent exceptions where exclusionary allegations have been upheld.

Although the number of cities which adopted zoning regulations grew from five in 1915 to 500 in 1925, a definitive court ruling on the constitutionality of zoning was not made until 1926 when the United States Supreme Court issued its opinion in the landmark case *Village of Euclid vs. Ambler Realty Co.* The court not only ruled that zoning was a valid exercise of the police power and as such denied injured parties compensation but also suggested that the court would liberally interpret the use of the police power for general land use planning.

The *Euclid* decision sparked the efforts of zoning advocates. From its original emphasis on safety and nuisances, the scope of zoning quickly expanded to the process of planning orderly community growth. Babcock states that from its modern inception, zoning was developed by "sophisticated and knowledgeable lawyers who believed the courts could be induced to permit municipalities, by an extension of the common law nuisance doctrine, to build a comprehensive regulatory scheme under the aegis of the police power" (1969, p. 4). The lawyers' belief became a reality with *Euclid*. It was a relatively simple task to draw use boundaries on a municipal street map, and a few pages of instructions took care of the simple requirements for permitted uses, yard dimensions, and maximum structure heights. To cope with cases of unfairness, municipalities were empowered to grant "variances" in instances of "hardship."

By the end of the 1930s, increasingly fine delineations of types of residential, commercial, and industrial activities were being utilized, e.g., single, multiple, and high-density, multiple-family residential zones. Within each of these categories specific regulations covering lot areas and dimensions, population density, and structural characteristics were added. However, not until the increasing suburban thrust following World War II did the basic structure of zoning—land districting—undergo significant modification.

To meet the challenges and complexities accompanying urbanization, municipalities required more flexibility in land use control. The old reliable variance was increasingly subject to judicial and professional criticism. To accommodate the need for flexibility, new techniques were required. First to appear was the special permit (also called conditional use or special exception). In succession, the floating zone, contract zoning, and planned unit development were also introduced. All permitted municipalities a great deal of discretion, including, if they wished, a means of working toward their individual goals of social homogeneity. These concepts, and zoning in general, have come under increasing attack by the courts and by professional writers on behalf of disadvantaged groups. In Babcock's view (1969, p. 3), despite all its subsequent embellishments, zoning's primary objective of protecting the neighborhood of single-family homes remains paramount. Although most discussions of zoning have focused on preservation of neighborhood property values, other benefits and costs of zoning should be considered in making a total economic evaluation.

A BENEFIT–COST FRAMEWORK FOR ZONING

This evaluation does not attempt to present new empirical evidence concerning the occurrence or degree of any benefit or cost. Rather, our objective is to construct a framework from material in Chapters 2 and 3 which identifies the major benefits and costs necessary for a complete economic evaluation of zoning regulations. Hypotheses about the potential benefits and costs of zoning will thus be generated, and existing evidence will be reviewed to ascertain the strength of each hypothesis. This procedure will provide a broader economic assessment of the zoning regulations currently employed in the United States than available previously.

As explained in Chapter 2, public control of land use may be desired on efficiency grounds for three objectives:

1. the reduction of negative external effects and the encouragement of positive external effects related to land use,
2. the provision of an optimal level of land-related public goods, and
3. the reduction of costs of providing certain public services.

On the other hand, the potential costs of zoning regulations include:

1. the costs of planning, administering, and implementing zoning regulations, and
2. the increased costs of residential, commercial, and industrial development due to the restrictiveness of zoning regulations.

The following sections explore the conceptual basis for each benefit and cost while reviewing existing evidence on occurrence and degree. This list of potential benefits and costs is not complete. Other, less apparent benefits and costs will be discussed later.

EXTERNAL EFFECTS

External effects originating from industrial nuisances and hazards provided the initial impetus for land-districting regulations. Today, the impetus is frequently the effects on residential neighborhoods of other types of residential structures and commercial or industrial activities. Reducing negative external effects and encouraging positive external effects are often two sides of the same coin.[4] Restricting multiple-family housing and its associated negative effects from a moderate or high-value single-family residential area, for example, provides a more esthetically satisfying neighborhood for existing residents and often increases their property values.

Why is there recourse to public action instead of deferral to the private land market when external effects exist in uncontrolled private land use? Restrictive covenants and nuisance litigation are techniques available to private parties for dealing with external land use effects. However, for two related reasons the private market is replaced by public regulation to modify external effects. First, the transaction costs necessary for organizing all affected parties and obtaining their collective agreement on individual benefit and cost responsibilities can be so great as to preclude private action.[5] Transaction costs become especially important as the size and heterogeneity of affected groups increase and as the identification and measurement of external benefits and costs are clouded by their inherent nature. Second, the elimination of many external effects produces, in effect, a public good for which a problem of nonexclusion occurs. That is, since one party's consumption of the desirable effect does not subtract from any other party's enjoyment, freeloaders will claim no benefit but cannot be excluded from enjoying the desirable effect.[6] For example, a quiet, esthetically appealing neighborhood is available to all residents at the same level; it is a public good.

External effects result from the interdependence of production and/or consumption processes. Figure 5.1 displays the intratemporal land use interactions when initiating and receiving parties are distinguished. An extreme example of the producer–producer type is the location of a factory that emits harmful gases next to a botanical nursery. Introduction of high-density, multiple-family housing into a

4. Clawson (1971, pp. 177–179) suggests a separate emphasis on positive external effects obtainable from zoning.

5. For a clear conceptual exposition of the effect of transaction costs and liability rules on market solutions to externality problems and implications for public policy, see Randall (1972). Randall generally characterizes transaction costs as the costs of resolving situations where involved parties have conflicting interests (including market transactions) and includes the costs of gathering information determining a bargaining position and strategy, arriving at a group decision (e.g., bargaining, negotiating, arbitration, adjudication), and enforcing the decision made.

6. This phenomenon represents a combination of the external effect and public good efficiency criteria presented in Chapter 2. A separation of benefit categories is used in this evaluative framework because correction of the external effect and public good problems may require different types of public action.

Receiver \ Initiator	Producer	Consumer
Producer	Interdependent production processes	Producer's input–output levels dependent on consumption activities
Consumer	Consumption activities dependent upon producer's input–output levels	Interdependent consumption activities

Figure 5.1. Potential external effects of land use activities.

low-density, single-family neighborhood is a commonly cited example of the consumer–consumer type. The location of a service station within or adjoining a residential neighborhood illustrates the producer–consumer type.

Davis (1963, p. 376) explains that in considering the possible combinations of positive and negative external effects in a two-party case, two types are of interest to zoning regulations. One is the case where party A creates a positive external effect for B but B has a negative effect on A. Given a choice, B is motivated to locate adjacent to A, but such a choice by B imposes a capital loss on A. A relevant example is the location of "expensive" (A) and "inexpensive" (B) residential dwellings. The second case is one where party A is neutral with respect to B but B has a negative external effect on A. If other considerations warrant it, B might locate next to A thus imposing a capital loss on A. An example would be a single-family residence (A) and a gasoline station (B).

Every production process and every resident's preferences are probably affected by innumerable external effects. An associate's cigar smoke or your neighbor's water fountain or a merchant's storefront lighting all may be things you do not like, but you probably would not pay to alter them. As explained in Chapter 2, economic efficiency provides a relatively unambiguous criterion for judging which external effects should be modified by zoning regulation: those which, when modified, allow for an increase in one party's utility while leaving the other affected individual utilities at the same level. Unfortunately, in many instances where zoning regulations make one party better off, another is made worse off. Such a situation is still not indeterminant.

If the person whose utility has decreased can be compensated (from the beneficiaries' gains) enough to restore his original utility level while leaving the beneficiaries better off than before, the modification can still be judged as an efficiency improvement, a social dividend so to speak.

Before evaluating the performance record of zoning in reducing external effects, we might ask what objectionable characteristics zoning regulations are designed to treat. The list surely would include air and water pollution, excessive noise levels, traffic congestion, esthetic disamenities, and social class separation (although the last is never explicitly stated). But zoning regulations do not directly address these external effects; instead, control is exercised over the location of various types of residential, commercial, and industrial activities, along with site and building characteristics and the density of population for each land use district. Functionally then, zoning has approached the amelioration of negative external effects by using surrogate or indirect criteria. The success of this approach depends on the correlation between external effects and the controlled characteristics judged to cause the external effects. In the next section we review some evidence relating to this correlation.

The Existence and Degree
of External Effects

Although commercial and industrial activities are surely subject to harmful external effects from other commercial, industrial, and even residential activities, the economics literature has attempted only to measure the influence of external effects on residential properties.[7] Therefore, of necessity, the following discussion will concentrate on the existence and degree of residential external effects.

Conceptually, at least, two classes of residential external effects can be distinguished (Mills 1976, pp. 27 40). The first pertains to the effect of nonresidential activities on residential property values. The impairment of residential property values usually results from the location of nonresidential activities and is, therefore, capitalized into the land-value component. The second class of externalities includes the effects of one residential activity on other residential uses. Restricting multiple-family uses and small-floor-area housing from large-lot single-family residential areas are common examples of actions to cope with this problem. These external effects are also usually capitalized into land values. For instance, a vacant residential lot in an area with

7. For excellent discussions of the conceptual nature of external effects addressed by zoning regulations and a survey of research results attempting to document the occurrence and magnitude of these effects, see Stull (1975) and Mills (1976).

considerable multiple-family housing is probably worth less than a similar vacant lot in an exclusively single-family neighborhood. Zoning treats these residential external effects by a combination of spatial separation, site and building regulations, and population density controls.

If zoning regulations effectively reduce negative external effects, the value of zoned residential property (land and/or structures) should exceed the value of the same property in the absence of zoning. Ideally, assessment of zoning's performance could be accomplished by measuring the change in property values from before to after zoning regulations. However, residential property values are affected by many factors other than zoning regulations, and to isolate the effect of zoning these factors must be held constant or controlled. Most studies have attempted to measure the influence of external effects by comparing property values of residential areas with varying degrees of external effects while controlling for other significant influences which also vary over the areas being analyzed.

The value of any residential property depends, in general, upon two separate sets of factors. The first consists of characteristics specific to the structure and the land: floor area, type of construction, lot size, accessibility to employment and retail centers, zoning classification, condition of neighborhood, quality of public services, specific property-tax rates, etc. The second set is not specific to the residential property but affects area property values in general: the area's population and economic growth rates, housing subsidies, the overall restrictiveness of zoning regulations for particular types of land and housing, etc. Since the latter set of factors affects all property values more or less equally, measuring the importance of external effects concentrates on specifying the influence of the first set.

A set of residential property value determinants can be constructed by first separating land and structure influences. Brigham (1965, p. 325) reasoned that land values are affected by five factors specific to a site, including

P = accessibility (e.g., miles to central business district)
A = amenities (e.g., absence of nonresidential uses)
T = topography (e.g., slope, drainage)
U = use classification (e.g., residential, commercial, industrial)
H = historical factors which affect utilization (e.g., location of major highways).

These factors describe influences on the value of equal-sized parcels of land in an undeveloped state. When structures are added to the land, the following variables also become important:

L = lot size (e.g., square feet)
S = public services (e.g., sewer, water, paved access)
F = structure size (e.g., floor area)
C = structure condition (e.g., age of dwelling unit).

Of course, other characteristics of the structure, such as number of rooms and presence of a garage, can affect the property value, but this list will serve for illustrative purposes. Denoting the value of the residential property as W, we can summarize the influences on any residential property in functional form as

$$W = f(P, A, T, U, H, L, S, F, C). \tag{5.1}$$

Most studies have attempted to account for the influence of external effects by specifying different levels of amenities (A) for the residential properties under analysis. That is, the elimination of negative external effects may be viewed as increasing the level of amenities. By controlling for or holding constant the remaining influences, the importance of external effects can be identified and measured.

Increasing external effect levels (or decreasing amenity levels) can be measured in various ways. If interest is centered on the value of individual parcels of property, then external effects can be measured as the distance to "incompatible" uses or the presence of "offensive" influences, such as a high volume of traffic through a neighborhood. When data are aggregated by community blocks or census tracts, measures of the influence of external effects on average property values include the proportion of "incompatible" uses within the blocks or census tracts and the presence of other "offensive" characteristics. Other external effects not directly related to zoning regulations, such as degree of crowding, racial composition, and state of housing disrepair, may also be included by appropriate specification.

As one might expect with the measurement of such a complex process as the influence of external effects on land values, there is conflicting evidence. Two studies of the single- and two-family dwelling market in Pittsburgh revealed similar results. Crecine et al. (the Crecine study) performed the first analysis in 1967. Their results indicated that the external effects hypothesized by zoning regulations to exert negative influences on single-family dwelling values, in fact, occurred randomly and had no systematic impact on land values. Not only did the magnitude of the external effects vary across zoning districts but also many effects were positive when expected to be negative. Although the data and procedures were far less than ideal, these preliminary results raised doubts about the stated intentions of zoning regulations to reduce external land use effects.

Reuter (1973) followed the Crecine study with an expanded and refined analysis of the Pittsburgh residential market. The period under analysis was expanded to 1958–1969, compared with 1958–1963 for the Crecine study. Explanatory factors were added to account for the influence of the physical characteristics of a property, e.g., slope, and building height. Two separate classifications of external effects addressed by zoning regulations were included: percentage of neighborhood area occupied by incompatible uses and other indicators of external effects such as building height and public land uses. The definition of a neighborhood was varied from 150 feet, as defined by the zoning ordinance, to 300 feet. Also, both single- and two-family residential markets were analyzed. Although inconsistencies between zoning's objectives and the presence of external effects were again revealed, Reuter's results showed a larger number of significant external effects than the Crecine study. However, closer examination revealed that the nonrandom effects were both positive and negative whereas the zoning ordinance predicted all negative. These effects had two characteristics in common: each applied to the single-family districts alone and each was from an analysis which used the 150-foot definition of a neighborhood as specified in the Pittsburgh zoning ordinance. Two suppositions were drawn from these results: first, a zoning ordinance may accurately specify the geographic area over which certain neighborhood attributes impose negative external effects, although it fails to identify the particular features that produce these effects; second, since two-family dwelling analyses did not exhibit significant effects, the geographic area significantly affected by external effects may not be constant over different land uses (e.g., residential, commercial, industrial) or factors inducing external effects (e.g., shopping center, factory, neighborhood store).

Reuter concluded that there is little likelihood that *all* of the negative external effects anticipated by a zoning ordinance will actually occur in urban property markets. This is not to say that the neighborhood of a dwelling is unimportant as a location variable, but it does suggest that unless there is considerable agreement about desirable and undesirable features, buyers will minimize the potential adverse effects in their own housing market selection process.

Although the results of the Crecine and Reuter studies are less than supportive of the existence of pervasive external effects, it is difficult to draw explicit conclusions. Problems in study design make each an incomplete test of the existence and degree of residential external effects as specified in the zoning ordinance. Neither study took individual structure characteristics into account, although most studies of residential property values have shown them to be among the most important determinants of dwelling value. Also, because of the nature of the census and land use data used, the Crecine study was forced to define a "neighborhood" as the city block in which a parcel was located with no reference to activities occurring directly across the street. Reuter improved this concept by including all parcels within a given distance of a dwelling. However, each study tested the hypothesis by sampling properties within only a small area, thus ignoring the variations among neighborhoods.

With the above problems in mind, Stull (1975) tested the external effect hypothesis for the Boston suburban area. To avoid the problem of sampling within neighborhoods and therefore ignoring inter-neighborhood effects, his sample consisted of 40 suburban municipalities in the Boston area. Each municipality is represented in the analysis by a set of medians or averages for the value of owner-occupied dwelling units, physical structure characteristics, accessibility to employment center, public services, and environmental characteristics, i.e., the external effects supposedly addressed by zoning regulations. These external effects were measured as the proportion of multiple-family, commercial, industrial, or institutional land uses within each municipality.

Stull's results were uniform. All external effects addressed by zoning regulations showed significant effects upon the median value of dwelling units.[8] For example, as the proportion of community land in industrial uses increased from 0% to 50%, the median value of an owner-occupied dwelling decreased by approximately $3570. Of singular interest was the finding that the proportion of commercial land had a positive effect on dwelling value for proportions up to 5% reflecting a convenience factor, the negative effect above that reflecting disamenity considerations. "In conclusion then, the data seem to reveal that in the study area, households were fairly sensitive to the land use environments of the communities in which they purchased homes" (Stull 1975, p. 551).

Each of the empirical measures of the importance of certain external effects derived by these three studies reflects implicit values of certain environmental characteristics *for one market at a particular time.* These values will surely vary among metropolitan areas and over periods of time. For example, if a particular residential area with high levels of commercial activity has residents who discount homes located in intensively commercial areas, one would expect a significant incremental value for homes in noncommercial areas. However, if the proportion of commercial activity decreases as time passes and the number

8. Although the practice of grouping individual observations within each neighborhood allows comparison across neighborhoods, the resulting significance tests are commonly less reliable than those for ungrouped data.

of residents who discount commercial activity also declines, the value of homes in noncommercial areas could decrease relative to the value of those in commerical areas. The importance of negative external effects depends upon the distribution of tolerance for the "offensive" activity among residents, i.e., demand, and the relative amount of the activity in the municipal area, i.e., supply. Both determinants will vary over time and space.

Other studies have addressed the importance of external effects on residential property values but only indirectly. Kain and Quigley (1975, pp. 190–230) found that the presence of commercial and industrial activity on parcel's block face had a significant negative effect upon apartment rents and single-family home values, but the study did not control for dwelling quality variation. Harris et al. (1968) and Weiand (1973) isolated similar effects of industrial and commercial activities.

All these studies attempted to identify and measure the influence of certain activities thought to exert negative external effects upon single-family homes. This was largely accomplished by measuring the degree of an "offensive" use in a neighborhood and then determining its influence on the price of single-family dwellings. How does this procedure relate to the effectiveness of zoning? If some studies fail to document significant negative effects, might this not imply that zoning regulations have eliminated the most offensive uses? Possibly, but all three study areas were characterized by "nonconforming" uses which, in theory, should exert some negative influences on single-family dwelling values. However, it is even more important that if all three studies had documented significant influence by "offensive" land uses on single-family dwelling values, there is no guarantee that zoning ordinances will eliminate them now or forever.

Can Zoning Eliminate External Effects?

Complaints are often registered that zoning bends in response to economic incentives, thus altering the "comprehensive land use plan." Many discretionary devices are available to permit this bending—variances, exceptions, temporary uses, floating zones, and planned unit developments. Thus planners may identify the potential negative external effects accurately, but planning commissions and city councils may alter plans when confronted with well documented "needs" for change. Siegan (1972, pp. 75–76) contends that the fact that Dallas, a zoned city, closely resembles Houston, an unzoned city, is evidence of the effective restraint of zoning on the location of "incompatible" land uses. He maintains that natural economic forces will encourage separation of uses even without zoning and that when these forces do not guarantee separation, either individual property owners will enter into agreements, such as restrictive covenants,[9] or specific land use ordinances will be passed to deal with the problem. Delafons (1969), on the other hand, believes that the reason zoned and unzoned cities develop alike is largely the emergence of private agreements that substitute for such public regulation as zoning.

Evidence on the dilemma is mostly subjective. Clawson (1971, p. 76) and Siegan (1972, pp. 75–76) concur on the importance of neighborhood homogeneity for zoning to be effective in reducing negative external effects. In essence, zoning is more effective in areas where homogeneous groups can fight off changes but may yield to economic pressures where there are no such groups.

Finally, one negative external effect important to some more homogeneous suburbs is never stated in the zoning ordinance: the introduction of low-income groups and/or different races. King and Mieszkowski (1973) determined that neighborhood boundary areas in New Haven exhibited a differential in rents of approximately 7% based on racial discrimination that reflected whites' taste for segregation from partly black areas. If zoning can be effectively utilized for racial or class segregation in such neighborhoods, then property values may increase but legal and moral questions of exclusion arise.

Implications for Reducing External Effects with Zoning

Assessing the effectiveness of zoning in reducing external effects requires two separate steps. First, it is necessary to document the existence of negative external effects in the residential housing market. Evidence about this is always site-specific. The Crecine and Reuter studies could not support the hypothesis that the Pittsburgh single- and two-family residential housing market was pervaded by negative external effects. However, Reuter concluded that the definition of a neighborhood adopted by zoning regulations, i.e., less than 150 feet from a residence, was relevant to the identification of potential negative external effects. Although it focused on variations between rather than within neighborhoods, Stull's analysis of the Boston metropolitan area showed that all negative external effects addressed by zoning regulations exerted significant influences on the value of single-family dwellings. The Stull study can be considered an improvement over the former studies since it took account of the influences of physical dwelling characteristics, level of public services, and accessibility to the central business district. Other studies have indirectly identified sig-

9. However, the successful introduction of restrictive covenants depends on the scale of individual development projects. Small developers cannot effectively sell the protection of restrictive covenants if they build only three houses in a project surrounded by apartment buildings.

nificant external effects on the value of single-family dwellings from commercial and industrial uses.

The second step requires an evaluation of whether zoning mitigates significant negative external effects when they appear. The evidence here is primarily subjective and indicates that only established homogeneous neighborhoods can effectively resist the introduction of "incompatible" uses. Where neighborhoods are not effectively organized, zoning may bend to the economic incentives of the marketplace with the aid of variances, special exceptions, floating zones, and planned unit developments.

A complete assessment of the efficiency of zoning regulations in reducing external effects would go one step beyond the studies reviewed above. Even if the existence of negative external effects is documented and it is also assumed that zoning can effectively reduce these effects, it should not be inferred that zoning achieves an *efficient* level of reduction. From an efficiency perspective, not all external effects should be eliminated.[10] Some represent cases where no "gains from trade" can be achieved. Ideally, zoning or any other method of public control of land use should be used to accomplish just that level of externality reduction where all possibilities for further "gains from trade" have been eliminated.

In this regard, if zoning regulations as originally implemented are too restrictive (i.e., lead to a more extensive reduction of external effects than is justified on efficiency grounds) variances, exceptions, and planned unit developments are techniques administrators can use to relax the restrictiveness and allow land use changes that encourage efficiency improvements. However, Merrifield (1965) concluded that not all rules or criteria utilized for granting zoning variances can be justified on the basis of improvements in economic welfare. There also remains the possibility that administrators may grant zoning changes in response to private pressure without weighing the associated benefits and costs.

PUBLIC GOODS

Recent concern over such land-related public goods as the preservation of open spaces, critical environmental areas, and agricultural production capacity, has suggested a broader role for public planning of land use. The characteristics of these goods deserve a brief review. Most importantly, they are goods of which, once they are produced, one person's consumption does not diminish the quantity left for others—joint con-

10. See Chapter 2, note 3.

sumption goods. (Sharing a pleasant view with your neighbor does not detract from your own enjoyment.) Attempts to distribute such public goods by charging the beneficiaries will necessarily misallocate consumption, since one person's consumption does not require a sacrifice from others. Yet a zero price will surely not entice private resources into public goods production.

Although extending zoning to provide such public goods would be a significant departure from traditional uses and raises serious distributive and legal questions, e.g., the "taking issue" (Bossellman, Callies, and Banta 1973), the potential efficiency of zoning for this purpose should also be analyzed. Is zoning capable of selecting the appropriate public goods and their optimal quantities?

Upon reflection, few examples of "pure" public goods will come to mind. Many goods are predominantly "public," but this characteristic is of concern to only a portion of the *total* population, and the rest are unaffected. This phenomenon is especially important in land use because many land-related public goods are locationally fixed, and thus, their actual benefits never equal potential benefits, since transportation costs restrict access (even view is ultimately restricted by the limitations of the human eye). Since the distribution of benefits is different for almost every land-related public good, the benefits and costs arising from them are difficult to estimate. Some examples will help to illustrate this point.

Provision of city parks is a case in point. The benefits of a city park are not distributed equally among the people. Knetsch (1962) concluded that land values next to a park are positively affected to degrees that depend on the extent residents and prospective residents want more parks than are supplied. Although difficult to measure, the increase in land values near a park should vary inversely with the distance from the park up to a threshold distance where potential value from the park vanishes. Placing a value on the benefits of a park is especially difficult when land values are not affected; since users are not excluded, preferences are not revealed. The social opportunity cost of providing a park is also difficult to assess. At a minimum, it is the value of the land in its best alternative use plus the cost of constructing and maintaining the park.

Preserving prime agricultural land as a public good is another appropriate example. The benefits may be regional, national, and even international: Given international markets, agricultural land preserved in one country today may benefit the entire world in the future. This potential time stream of benefits is extremely difficult to measure. Local benefits might include maintaining a varied job base (if the area is dependent on primary processing or transportation of agricultural products) or preserving open space. The social opportunity costs of preserving agricultural land (or decreasing its rate of conversion) would be, at a minimum, the value of the land in its best alternative use where development pressure is great, this will ultimately be reflected in the price of land for residential, commercial, and industrial uses.

The discussion of examples could continue, but we are concerned with the potential efficiency of zoning in providing such public goods. Zoning, as an exercise of the police power, is a means of direct regulation, and therefore, its economic efficiency in providing public goods lies squarely in the hands of local or state decision-makers and in the accuracy of their perception of the kind and degree of social benefits and costs. The social benefits will be the sum of the values each consumer puts on the public good in question, while the social costs must include the highest alternative value for the land plus direct costs of providing the good.[11]

What information and incentives do zoning administrators have in deciding about land-related public goods? One expects that potential benefits would be overstated since beneficiaries would be numerous and would not be required to pay for provision. On the other hand, since costs would be confined to a relatively few owners whose land would be restricted to provide goods and lose their development value, gainers would apparently outnumber losers. Moreover, if the land used for public goods reduces the supply of developable land, housing prices may increase more than they would without the public goods, but these costs are not likely to be recognized since their relationship to taking land for public use is not readily apparent. In short, zoning administrators have little information and few incentives for balancing the social benefits against the social costs. In fact, since potential benefits would be overstated and costs ignored, one would expect an "oversupply" of land-related public goods. If the land designated for public goods were owned by a municipality, administrators would at least be forced to take these potential benefits and costs into account for tax-revenue considerations. Modifications to traditional zoning regulations, such as transferable development rights and zoning by eminent domain, represent potential improvements in this regard since some beneficiaries of the public good are assessed and those providing land are compensated. The following two chapters will treat these modifications.

11. This, of course, does not consider the social desirability of the benefits and costs from a distributional perspective.

PUBLIC SERVICES

With the increasing recognition of the social costs attendant on municipal growth, more attention is being focused on controlling or covering the costs of providing various public services. This has led to two recent developments. First, some communities, most notably Ramapo, New York and Petaluma, California, have designed or tied their land use controls to the reduction of public service costs (Schnidman 1974). Second, an increasing number of communities are using various methods, e.g., special connection fees, taxes, public service dedications in lieu of fees, to shift the burden of additional public services to new residents who require them.

Irrespective of these two developments, the objectives of a zoning ordinance include both direct and indirect implications for the economic efficiency of providing public services. Direct implications arise from such objectives as to promote a safe, effective traffic system; to facilitate fire and police protection; or to provide adequate community facilities. Objectives with indirect implications include to provide a precise guide for physical development of the city or to prevent undue concentrations of population.

There seem to be three separate issues relating to the effects of zoning regulations on the costs of public services. First, zoning regulations can affect the development density of a community, the contiguity of development expansion (i.e., leapfrogging), and the "planning"[12] of individual developments, all of which in turn can affect the costs of providing required public services such as streets, water, and sewerage facilities. Second, zoning regulations can be used to direct development so that the existing or planned public service infrastructure (e.g., water or sewage treatment facilities) are used to capacity but not over- or underutilized. Finally, some have suggested that such land use controls as zoning might be used to restrict residential areas to persons or families with similar demands for public services, especially educational facilities. Each of these three issues will be discussed in turn.

Effects of Zoning on Development Density, Contiguity, and "Planning"

If the objectives of zoning were solely minimizing the cost of public services, the resultant plan would cluster all development closely

---

12. "Planning" as used here refers to the internal contiguity of structures within an individual development. See Real Estate Research Corporation (1974) for a full description of "planning."

around a central public service supply with density of development decreasing as distance increases. Furthermore, there would be no leap-frogging and each individual development would be planned for maximum internal contiguity. Obviously, zoning has not done this. Zoning authorities recognize that the demand for residential, commercial, and industrial sites depends on more than minimal public service costs. The following discussion of the performance and potential of zoning for cost reduction will assume that the initial capital outlays for public service capacity and infrastructure are distributed on an average cost basis. Given this assumption, the relevant questions for this efficiency analysis are (1) how has zoning affected the costs of public services in the past? and (2) what potential does it have for affecting them in the future? A first step is to review the evidence about which development characteristics significantly influence public service provision costs.

Probably the most comprehensive effort to estimate the variability of public service costs for different neighborhood and community types was made by the Real Estate Research Corporation (1974). This anzlysis generated cost figures for prototype developments rather than identifying variations in cost for existing developments. The approach assumed typical site conditions (e.g., slope and drainage) and an absence of any public service infrastructure and then, using standard unit cost figures, estimated the costs of building at different densities and with different degrees of "planning" (i.e., internal contiguity). The public services analyzed included schools, streets and roads, sewers, water, storm drainage, police and fire protection, solid waste collection, libraries, health care, and general government. Results of the study showed a surprising consistency in that "planning," to a limited extent, but increasing densities, to a more significant extent, result in lower costs for provision of the public services. Therefore, while planning results in cost savings, density is a much more influential cost determinant. The study also emphasized that its conclusions apply only to public service costs and ignore questions of personal preference for and revenues generated from different types of development.

Although it is interrelated with the effect of density, the effect of distance on the costs of providing public services was not separately addressed by the study. Some evidence on this subject is available from less comprehensive studies. Downing (1973) developed synthetic cost estimates of the variance of sewer collection and treatment costs with distance. For instance, he found that, holding density constant at 1.0 person per acre, the marginal annual cost per capita varies from $66 at 5 miles to $301 at 30 miles. As the evidence suggests, one might expect some economies of distance, i.e., as distance increases 500%, costs increase 356%, but, in general, public service provision costs increase with distance.

Gibbs (1973) estimated the effect of distance on sewage transmission costs using actual data from Washington County, Oregon. His results on the effects of distance and contiguity are summarized in the following statement.

> As distance of residence from the site of sewage treatment increases, it was shown that the cost of sewage transmission increases. For a given distance, the cost per unit of distance increases as population density falls. Consequently, contiguous expansion of the urban fringe is less costly than discontiguous expansion, and high density discontiguous expansion is less costly than low density contiguous expansion. For example, for a 500-acre sub-basin located 10 miles distant from the site of sewage treatment, the cost of sewage transmission decreases from $1286.59 to $18.00 per household as population density increases from 1 to 100 persons per acre. Recent low density expansion of the suburban fringe in discontiguous tracts is, therefore, high-cost expansion (1973, p. 109).

Assuming that the price of public services has not been fully sensitive to density, contiguity, and "planning" in most municipalities, we can now analyze some general effects of zoning on the costs of public services. First to come to mind are density controls; minimum lot sizes, limits on the number of housing units per acre, yard requirements, and open space ratios. All these controls tend to decrease population density and, therefore, increase the costs of public services.[13] Their effects on contiguity and "planning" are impossible to generalize; they will depend upon the way individual communities plan, enforce, and implement their zoning ordinances. Although not discussed above, other required improvements such as streets, sidewalks, and storm drains defined by the subdivision regulations will also increase public service costs above the minimum to the extent the minimum standards are above the equilibrium levels desired by community residents.

Zoning Regulations and Public Service Infrastructure

Although potentially important, zoning's ability to aid in the optimal utilization of existing or planned public service infrastructure has received little attention. Reuter (1973, p. 337) suggests that compelling

---

13. It is interesting to note the conflicting efficiency effects in this regard, since density controls are usually thought of as externality-abating controls. Also to be noted is the potential complementarity in using zoning to increase contiguity (and thus decrease public service costs) and provide open space as a public good.

the segregation of high-density and low-density land uses might permit a municipality to limit construction of projects requiring large-scale public investments to high-density regions and economize on these expenditures in low-density areas. For example, increased density could be allowed in areas where public service capacity already exists or restricted where capacity is fully utilized. No evidence other than speculation is available to determine whether zoning has furthered or inhibited this potential source of savings.

Zoning Regulations and Homogeneous Demands for Public Services

The two issues discussed above address questions of cost efficiency for public services. This section examines the contention that under an efficient jurisdictional arrangement all residents of the jurisdiction consume the same amount (value) of housing, pay the same local taxes, and consume the optimum amount of local government services, just financed by tax receipts.[14] Introduction of lower-value housing would allow some residents to pay lower taxes while enjoying the same level of public services as residents who pay higher taxes. A variety of institutional considerations, such as federal subsidies to education and the limited number of local jurisdictions offering homogeneous packages of public services, limit applicability of this notion in the real world. The important questions, however, are (1) can zoning regulations be used to promote the efficient consumption of public services? and (2) if so, to what extent have they been employed in this manner?

To achieve efficiency in consumption, zoning must be able to construct jurisdictions, so to speak, with similarly valued housing. A variety of controls are available to accomplish this task: lot size requirements, limitations on multiple-family dwellings, and floor area requirements are among the more important examples. Implementation of these techniques to restrict the value of homes in a jurisdiction has often been referred to as "fiscal" or "exclusionary" zoning.[15]

According to Clawson (1971) and Seigan (1972), the effectiveness of these exclusionary techniques is highest in homogeneous, single-family suburbs. In Mills' opinion (1976, p. 46), most relatively new American suburbs show substantial evidence of Tiebout-like influences. Central cities and older residential areas which often lack the power to exclude with zoning because of the existing diversity of land uses, are frequently too large to meet demands for government

14. See Mills (1976, p. 42). This contention is related to the Tiebout hypothesis. For those interested in a clear conceptual statement of the hypothesis, see Hamilton (1975).
15. This concept will be treated in greater detail below in the discussion of zoning's distributive effects.

services from small groups of residents. It is important to remember that even though zoning regulations may provide some efficiency benefits to exclusionary suburbs, the indirect effects of exclusionary zoning can impose costs on other groups of residents and may not be desirable on equity grounds.

Implications for Reducing Public Service Costs with Zoning

The issues reviewed above involve the potential economic benefits of utilizing zoning to provide public services. The evidence on the influence of contiguity and density suggests that using zoning to influence the locations and types of development encouraged might be most beneficial. In this regard, the increasing acceptance and popularity of planned unit developments is interesting. Lower public service costs may be an important stimulus to this trend. Babcock and Bosselman (1973, p. 73) contrasted the linear distances of seven public services between conventional subdivision regulations and planned unit developments (PUD) in Devner. The reduction in footage for the PUDs is significant. The use of zoning to utilize existing and planned public service infrastructure optimally appears to be an important potential benefit, but little evidence exists for judgment. Promoting efficient consumption of public services through exclusionary zoning may offer benefits to some types of neighborhoods, but it can also generate costs for other groups.

Nothing would cause voters to pressure for zoning that achieves optimal allocations and levels of public services if an average cost pricing scheme is employed, since service consumers (voters) do not pay marginal costs. Perhaps reliance on pricing schemes that allocate the cost of public services to those who use them while allowing potential residents to choose the types, densities, and locations of development they want is a better alternative. The trend toward shifting the costs of public services to those who require them is encouraging in this regard.

TRANSACTION COSTS

Planning, implementing, and administering a zoning ordinance can require substantial outlays from many parties.[16] Taxpayers must pay for the planning department. Homeowner associations must devote time and resources to fight "undesirable" land uses introduced by zoning changes. Developers must hire legal and other professional services to present their cases for rezoning property for development.

---

16. See note 5 for a definition of transaction costs.

The level of transaction costs for zoning regulations will, in general, depend upon two factors. First, and most basically, they will be determined by the extensiveness (ambitiousness) of land use control goals (e.g., the desired degree of external effect reduction and public goods provision) to be achieved through zoning. In turn, a jurisdiction's population and political structure will affect the establishment of these goals and, therefore, the nature and size of the organizational and administrative structure necessary to carry out the zoning process. Second, the assignment of responsibilities for undertaking action by particular parties or groups in response to land use control policies will affect the level of transaction costs. Diverse heterogeneous groups will, in general, experience much higher costs in mobilizing to pursue a common goal while small homogeneous groups, such as some public agencies or neighborhood associations, will require less time and fewer resources to organize effectively.

To faciliate the discussion of transaction costs, the zoning process can be divided into four more or less distinct phases: (1) planning, (2) decision-making, (3) amendments and change, and (4) implementation [Siegan 1972, pp. 1–19; Barlowe 1972, pp. 541–545].[17] The transaction costs of each phase will be discussed in turn.

Planning

The first phase consists of drafting a zoning ordinance and map showing the boundaries of the districts or zones within which different regulations apply. The ordinance usually contains six sections: (1) a statement of purposes, (2) general provisions, including definitions of terms and regulations for nonconforming uses, (3) identification and boundary descriptions of the different land use districts, (4) the regulations for each district, (5) provisions for administration and enforcement, and (6) provisions for changes and amendment. Municipalities of different sizes perform this task in different ways. Large cities usually assign it to their planning departments and/or hire private consultants or appoint special commissions. Smaller towns or villages may hire professional planning firms to draft both documents if they do not have permanent planning departments.

Although there is no standard procedure for performing this step, it usually begins with a survey of land uses and physiography for all land in the jurisdiction. After this is done, there is a great deal of diversity. It can be an enormously complex task for a larger city since its area is larger, its population more diverse, its life styles (and thus its objectives) more varied. A list of possible considerations might include, for

17. Although zoning is depicted here as a sequential process, the occurrence of different phases will depend on the type of change considered, e.g., original ordinance, rezone, variance, general amendment.

every location, use compatibility, economic feasibility, property values, existing uses, adjoining and nearby uses, traffic, topography, utilities, schools, future growth patterns, conservation, and environment. The cost of studying the economic feasibility of one use at one location for one period could be thousands of dollars. Ascertaining the preferences of the residents is costly; market surveys can be too expensive. There is also the problem of coordination with bordering municipalities. Because a huge number of factors affect drafting the official map (with associated regulations) and there is no guide to assign rankings in importance, the planner is often allowed much leeway. His judgment may reduce the transaction costs associated with planning, but it may also increase errors in specifying the effects of land use planning.

Decision-Making

Public participation is an integral part of the adoption of an ordinance or its general amendments. The ordinance constructed during the planning phase must go through formal public hearings, and, therefore, much informal discussion. First, the zoning commission holds a public hearing at which affected property owners can voice their opinions. Some attention is directed to the ordinance text, but most is focused on the official map indicating land use district boundaries. After its first presentation to the public, the proposal will generate varying degrees of public and private activity. Property owners who interpret their zoning classification as a negative influence on property value may consult elected representatives and planning officials. After the zoning commission submits its final report to the local governing body, a second set of public hearings must be advertised and held. Following these hearings, local government is free to debate and accept or reject the proposed ordinance.

Transaction costs incurred during this phase vary with the scale and complexity of the proposed ordinance, i.e., the size of the jurisdiction, the degree of change from preexisting land use patterns, and the degree of differentiation of land use categories. Other transaction costs include those associated with organizing interest groups and coalitions which tend to increase with the number and heterogeneity of such groups.

Amendments and Change

Comprehensive or general amendments to a zoning ordinance are rarely proposed, but petitions for change of specific parts are common. These include variances, special permits or exceptions, floating zones, conditional zones, and planned unit developments. A variance is a license issued to a landowner by an administrative agency (for instance, a board of zoning appeals) to construct a structure or carry out an activity not permitted under the general regulations. A special permit (also called conditional use or exception) also licenses development or use in conflict with the zoning ordinance, but in this case the discretion vested in the licensing agency is more circumscribed than with variances. Floating zones are districts set up by the zoning ordinance but not initially mapped to a particular location. The regulations spell out circumstances that must exist before a landowner can apply and set forth performance standards that enable individualized treatment of details. Conditional zoning reclassifies a single applicant's property to another zoning district while imposing certain conditions to ameliorate the impact of the new use on neighboring properties. This device allows a greater degree of incremental decision-making than floating zoning. The newest technique to change zoning classifications is the planned unit development (PUD). Developed to cope with the inflexible individual-lot approach of most zoning regulations, the PUD is employed when a developer wishes to develop a relatively large piece of property, usually 10 acres or more. Traditional articles of the zoning ordinance (height, bulk, open space) do not strictly apply, but the overall plans must be reviewed and accepted by the zoning commission.

"Thousands of petitions are filed annually and many more thousands of citizens become involved in their disposition" (Siegan 1972, p. 11). Each petition for change usually causes transaction costs on both sides. Those introducing the petition may hire professionals (lawyers, engineers, economists) to prepare their case, thus adding costs. Property owners who oppose the change may attempt to organize. If the groups are large and heterogeneous, the costs of forming a coalition may be high. Unfortunately, such costs may be incurred repeatedly since many property owners fight a recurring battle to protect their zoning rights from being watered down by variances. Those unhappy with a zoning body's decision can seek judicial redress although there are limitations to obtaining relief in the courts (Siegan 1972, p. 17). Any potential plaintiff has to be willing to spend the considerable time and money necessary to carry a case to a higher appellate level, and even when the facts are favorable, the most affluent plaintiff may find such litigation an unreasonable risk.

Transaction costs in this phase will vary with (1) the number of petitions presented for change, (2) the type of change proposed, e.g., a small variance is likely to cost less than a large planned unit development, and (3) the coalition costs of parties opposing change, i.e., the degree of heterogeneity. Fixed transaction costs are required for the board of appeals and other zoning administrative personnel regardless of the volume of petitions. It is interesting to speculate on the effect of altering the rules regarding zoning changes. If the administrative agency was responsible for demonstrating why a district or use should *not* change rather than requiring those requesting change to show why it should be allowed, the level of external effect elimination might also change. Currently those requesting changes must bear the brunt of the transaction costs, and thus their incentives for land uses that require zoning changes are tempered.

Implementation

Implementation includes the enforcement of the zoning ordinance and any attendant changes. In some cities the building inspector enforces the ordinance through issuance of building permits while larger cities may have zoning administrators to review permit requests. It is difficult to generalize about the degree of enforcement, but it is probably greater in large municipalities with larger and more competent staffs. However, some examples suggest that the degree depends upon the residents' degree of concern about violations. Smaller cities which cannot employ personnel for administration and enforcement usually operate informally. The greatest degree of enforcement may occur in affluent suburbs where vested interests and monetary resources encourage greater participation in enforcement.

Transaction costs for this phase should be low compared to those of previous phases: enforcement officials require a fixed component; other costs vary with the number of violations and subsequent degree of citizen participation. Even though the legal responsibility for identification of violations is placed on the public sector, it is likely that privately affected parties significantly influence the degree of enforcement. Policing costs are high if they fall on public officials and therefore they may wait until they receive citizen complaints.

Implications of Transaction Costs

Although most of the literature on zoning refers to its potentially significant transaction costs, a detailed analysis is not to be found. The prospect of expanding land use planning and the role of zoning should sharpen interest in the subject. Comprehensive land use planning based on zoning requires extensive documentation and citizen participation. Excessive transaction costs for drafting plans and for regulatory bodies or for interest groups could make such planning impractical. Also, the manner in which responsibilities for action are assigned to affected parties will influence the size of transaction costs and the degree of external effect abatement (Randall 1972).

A first step in documenting transaction costs under existing zoning regulations would be to analyze the public expenditures recorded in municipal budgets. The next step, one far more difficult, would be to measure the private costs attending the different phases. Particularly important here are costs associated with amendment and change. Because of suburban expansion pressures, an ordinance devised fifteen, ten, or even five years ago may no longer reflect "socially desired" land use allocations and intensities and require incremental change through variances, exceptions, or planned unit developments. In addition to substantial transaction costs for affected parties, other costs from delayed land use conversion may occur. The following section will analyze the influence of the latter on the costs of development.

COSTS OF DEVELOPMENT

Zoning regulations are often alleged to increase the costs of residential, commercial, and industrial development. The strength of this allegation depends on (1) the extent to which zoning regulations keep the amount of land and/or number of structures lower than they would be in an unregulated market and (2) the extent to which minimum land and structure characteristics, e.g., lot size, exceed the level they would otherwise reach. Earlier, it was suggested that zoning effectiveness varies between areas. In areas with effective groups interested in land use changes, a zoning classification can be a long and costly process. In areas without such groups, a zoning classification may be changed by showing a well-documented "economic need" or making an illicit payment to public officials. For this reason it is difficult to generalize about the record of zoning in restricting development. At a minimum, it can delay land conversion while landowners and interest groups incur short-run transaction costs. If it inhibits long-run market adjustments, its maximum effect will undoubtedly be lower quantities of land and housing which, in turn, will cause higher prices unless nearby areas abound where development may proceed without comparable zoning restrictions.

All types of development can be affected by zoning regulations, but most attention has centered on the costs of housing. Siegan (1972, p. 123) notes that zoning can also affect the amount of commercial or industrial development by "overzoning" or "underzoning." Both may cause the price of land to increase. "Overzoning," or zoning more land for a purpose than is needed, can lead to speculation and drive up prices of the over-zoned land. More commonly, "underzoning" is employed to limit the number of locations for commercial or industrial development. Although often overlooked, an indirect consequence of this type of restriction may be an increase in property taxes for residents since taxes on commercial or industrial developments often exceed the costs of public services required. Although effects of zoning on commercial and industrial development can be important, the present section will emphasize the effects on the costs of housing since the latter area has received the most intensive study.

Conceptually, at least, zoning can influence the costs of housing in three ways (Siegan 1972, pp. 95–96):

1. By controlling the total amount of land and the minimum area of lots, zoning may influence the supply and price of land for various residential uses. This price is reflected in the land component of housing.
2. Zoning may also influence rents and prices when it directly or indirectly reduces or enlarges the supply of different types of housing. This price is reflected in the structure component of housing.
3. Zoning may also include other requirements that add to the cost of land or construction, such as lot-size and garage requirements.

It is worth digressing for a moment to examine diagrammatically the conditions under which a reduction in the *short-run potential* supply of residential land affects the market price.[18] Assume that, because of the nature and use of zoning regulations, the short-run potential supply of land for residential use is effectively reduced from the supply without regulation. Depending on the level of market demand for the various uses, the price of land may rise above the level without regulation. This is illustrated in Figure 5.2. Assume we are referring to one type of residential land denoted as L, e.g., single-family residential, five miles from the central business district. Assume the initial market demand is defined by curve D_0D_0. Assume also that the unregulated supply of L is denoted by the curve S_0S_0 but that under zoning regulations for the jurisdiction, the short run limit is L^*S^*. Consequently, under zoning regulations the supply curve is S_0S^*. The price of L under initial conditions is given by the intersection of D_0D_0 and S_0S^*, or P_0. The limit defined by the zoning regulations has not affected the market price. Over time, if the market demand shifts to curve D_1D_1, the price now rises to P^*. Without the zoning limitation the price would be P_1. A similar analysis could illustrate the same effect on the price of the structure component of housing.

Therefore, the effect of density controls on the price of a type of land or housing depends on relative market demand in the short run. In the

18. Short-run and potential because in the long run, rezoning, variances, and special exemptions can occur, and the landowner is, of course, not forced to employ or sell his land for the most valuable use.

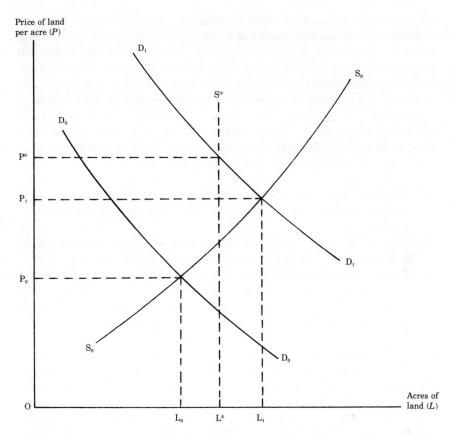

Figure 5.2. Potential price effects of zoning restricting total land supply.

long run, if economic growth and population increase, increased demand pressure may cause the short-run limit to be increased through techniques such as variances, rezoning, or special exceptions. However, the short-run price increases will accrue to the owners of land and/or housing and increase costs for those who wish to purchase them.

Zoning Influences on the Cost of Housing

As explained in the discussion of external effects, the value of a house, including land and structures, depends on both the characteristics specific to the house and neighborhood and the non-specific factors that affect the local area, state, region, or nation in general. To isolate the effect of zoning on the costs of housing apart from reducing external effects, it is necessary to establish controls for all other influences. Two approaches have been utilized in efforts to do this. The first is to collect actual data and then attempt to isolate statistically the influence of zoning. The second is to extrapolate the supply of housing presently embedded in zoning regulations and then compare it with projected housing "needs." These approaches will be discussed in turn.

Sagalyn and Sternlieb (1973) performed a statistical analysis of the impact of exclusionary land use and building controls on the price of new, single-family, tract homes. Data from 530 new house models and 153 subdivsions were collected from 19 out of 21 counties in New Jersey. The procedure was to explain the price of new homes by accounting for the influences of four sets of factors.

1. Public policy's incorporation of exclusionary controls commonly used to restrict new residential growth, e.g., lot size, lot frontage, setback.
2. Physical features and amenities of new houses, e.g., cinderblock, floor area, full basement, appliances.
3. Strong determinants of the market place, e.g., municipal density, municipal tax rate, housing stock.
4. The builder's scale of operation, e.g., the annual number of units constructed by the builder and size of subdivision development.

As the authors anticipated, public policy decisions pertaining to minimum zoning requirements were significant influences on the selling prices of new homes. However, they were not the most important. The size of the house was the single most important factor although, of course, size may be directly affected by minimum floor-area and lot-size requirements. Because of aggregation of all sample subdivisions, several expected effects of zoning and subdivision constraints were muted. The authors also note that the full impact of present zoning regulations on average lot size and lot frontage (thus land and housing supply) is difficult to measure because (1) there is a time lag between establishment of new zoning patterns and their translation into physical development, and (2) many builders choose first those land parcels with the smallest minimum lot-size and/or frontage requirements so that the full impact of these exclusionary practices is yet to affect the consumer.

Sagalyn and Sternlieb concluded that relaxing zoning regulations, i.e., making land available for higher-density, single-family units, would not provide housing for all income groups who desire it but cannot presently afford it. "However, changes in major zoning practices would appear to enlarge the effective housing market considerably, provided that builders made concomitant reductions in the size and amenities of housing offered" (Sagalyn and Sternlieb 1973, p. 69).

Reductions of lot size, lot frontage, and livable floor area to 15,000 square feet, 100 feet, and 1600 square feet respectively, along with relaxation of building codes yielded a predicted sales price of approximately $36,527, $12,481 lower than the $49,007 average.

Bergman (1974) used the second approach. The procedure employed was to determine the measurable dimensions (distribution) of the probable prices and rents of housing embedded in the narrative of a zoning ordinance and then compare them to the projected distribution of household incomes in the sample. The figures compared were no more than carefully prepared estimates, calculated for six townships in Delaware County, Pennsylvania. Although the results varied from one township to another, the overall conclusion was the same: present zoning ordinances will result in a substantial shortfall in housing for all income groups and drive housing prices up unless they are altered. The principal failing of this approach is that it assumed a great deal of certainty about zoning regulations over time which, according to most authors, may yield to various degrees if economic pressures build.

In a study of the causes of land price changes in the San Francisco Bay area, Maisel did not focus on the influence of zoning, but his results are applicable to the issue. He isolated three components of increases in the cost of land for housing (Maisel 1963, p. 228). The increase in raw land prices accounted for over 50%; the rise in costs of development and subdivision improvement standards accounted for 28%; and the increases in required lot sizes accounted for 20–25%. Obviously, the last two components are strongly influenced by the applicable zoning regulations.

OTHER BENEFITS AND COSTS OF ZONING

The five categories of benefits and costs discussed above may be viewed as some of the most important effects of zoning regulations, but they do not represent a total enumeration. It is worthwhile to review some other, less obvious influences.

If zoning eliminates external effects by spatial separation of "incompatible uses," excessive segregation of residential areas from employment and retail centers may lead to increased travel costs (Mills 1976, pp. 29–31). Obviously, the increased quantity and quality of road and transit systems have decreased the travel time due to separation and, therefore, the associated transportation costs. However, the complementarity between the goals of external effect elimination and desirable transportation systems should not ignore the requirements of providing a transportation infrastructure to achieve separation of "incompatible" uses. Since the benefits of a transportation system are much more varied than separation of "incompatible" land uses, only part of the costs should be attributed to zoning. Two relevant questions emerge: do zoning regulations effectively approximate private preference for segregation? If so, to what degree do they approach an optimum? (Mills 1976, pp. 29, 30).

If zoning regulations do provide greater certainty of land use patterns, private investment decisions relating to land and housing may be improved. For example, a homeowner may improve or at least maintain the quality of his residence if he has some assurance that a gasoline station will not be allowed on an adjacent lot.

Siegan (1972, p. 135) notes a potential cost of zoning in that competition in the real estate market may be reduced by restricting the entry of land and housing developers. In that case, those permitted entry will be able to charge higher prices, and/or offer poorer quality. For example, if the number of apartments in a community is held below the number that would be built without zoning, existing apartment owners may be able to charge higher rents and/or provide less maintenance.

THE DISTRIBUTION OF BENEFITS AND COSTS

As explained in Chapter 3, the social desirability of zoning cannot be assesed by evaluating only the existence and magnitude of its benefits and costs. Its effects on equity between groups is also of vital concern, i.e., the incidence of those benefits and costs by income, wealth, or other categories. Recent court cases, such as *South Burlington NAACP vs. Mt. Laurel Township* (New Jersey 1975), are in large part a reflection of this concern. Exclusion of lower-income or racial minority groups from certain municipalities has been the central issue. In some cases the effects of the zoning ordinance may be adjudged "inequitable."

A description of zoning's distributive effects, potential or realized, may therefore aid in assessing the desirability of any proposed expansion of zoning regulations. These effects may be generally defined as differential changes in the preregulation distribution of income and/or wealth due to price or quantity effects of zoning. Since little research has been conducted to document the incidence of zoning benefits and costs, the following sections will primarily outline potential effects.

External Effects

Two specific distributive effects may stem from efforts to eliminate harmful external effects with zoning regulations.[19] First, the act of

19. See Chapter 3 for the definition of and distinction between specific and general distributive effects.

defining use intensities for regulated properties in the jurisdiction may alter the geographical distribution of land values which would otherwise develop in an unregulated land market setting (Yeates 1965). Therefore, the public action of use districting has the potential of increasing property values for some owners, i.e., windfalls, while decreasing the value for others, i.e., wipeouts (Hagman 1975). This particular effect of zoning provides an incentive for landowners to appeal for increased use intensity from the appropriate public decision-making body. On this point, Clawson offers the following evalution:

> Zoning almost certainly affects land values, often greatly. The strenuous efforts made by developers, land speculators, and others to get zoning changed are sufficient evidence of the monetary gains to be achieved from rezoning. Real estate developers recognize that the kind of zoning (commercial as contrasted with residential) as well as specific zoning provisions, especially such matters as density of use and height of buildings, greatly affect the value of a tract of land. Some properties can be developed under one set of regulations but not under others. The building and developing trade is fully alert to the importance of zoning as affecting land values (1971, p. 184).

The uneven distribution of benefits and costs among landowners is thus a prime factor in getting zoning plans changed.

How are windfalls and wipeouts distributed among various classes?[20] Surely, applying for variances, exceptions, conditional uses, and the like is often spurred by potential economic gain. Usually to receive permission for increased intensity of development or avoid lower intensities, time and resources must be expended to present a case to the zoning decision-making body. If we assume that the same transaction cost is required from any property owner wishing to influence the zoning plan, we can expect that, holding other factors constant, the probability of receiving windfalls or avoiding wipeouts varies directly with income levels, since it will pay only the owners of larger or more valuable tracts to take action.

The second specific effect results from the ability of zoning regulations to enhance property values by spatially separating "incompatible" uses, the traditional justification for zoning. If the "undesirable" land uses restricted from a particular district do, in fact, represent relevant external effects, landowners should be willing to pay more for the absence of these effects. Consequently, the success of the zoning ordinance in correctly identifying and effectively reducing negative external effects should be reflected in increased land values. This is the

20. For an observation borne of personal experience see Raleigh (1964).

type of influence that Stull, Reuter, and Crecine et al. attempted to identify and measure.

The distribution of benefits from eliminating harmful external effects is probably quite diverse. One way to identify those who receive the greatest benefits under existing ordinances would be to identify the districts or neighborhoods where changes in zoning classifications or the introdution of "incompatible" uses have been blocked. We indicated above that neighborhoods with the greatest success are well-established, homogeneous, single-family housing districts (Clawson 1971, Siegan 1972). Although the lack of objective evidence constrains generalization, one suspects that such neighborhoods are not characterized by low-income residents. If for no other reason, this result could be expected from the role of transaction costs in avoiding zoning costs and receiving zoning benefits.

Public Goods

The use of zoning to provide certain public goods could also result in two specific distributive effects. First, properties near the public good may increase in value reflecting the consumptive value of the public good, i.e., a windfall. Second, property utilized for the public good may decrease in value reflecting the loss of development value, i.e., a wipe-out. As with external effect elimination, the distribution of benefits and costs associated with providing public goods is difficult to predict. To the extent that significant costs in time and resources are necessary to secure a specific benefit or avoid a specific cost from a public good, one might also expect that property owners with greater income or wealth would fare better.

Public Services

The distributive effects of using zoning to minimize the cost of public services are even more obscure than those related to public goods. If zoning did promote increased density and maximum contiguity, the costs of providing such public services as water and sewers would decrease. If we also assume that those on the urban fringe did not originally pay all public service costs associated with their location, the proportion subsidized by residents closer to the urban center would decrease with increasing density and contiguity. In addition, permitting increased density, e.g., eight-acre minimum lots instead of half-acre, would probably grant some windfalls but it is impossible to generalize about their distribution without specific plans for a specific location.

Transaction Costs

The costs of operating a planning department and other activities related to zoning are ultimately supported by the jurisdiction's tax revenues and their distribution, therefore, depends upon the regressiveness, progressiveness, or neutrality of the tax system. As suggested earlier, the most important transaction costs are probably those associated with amendments and changes of the zoning ordinance, any requests for which usually inspire action from both supporters and opponents. Like the distributive effects of public goods and public services, those of transaction costs are specific to individual landowners and therefore are impossible to generalize about. However, the rules that assign individual responsibilities regarding zone changes can be expected to greatly influence the incidence of specific costs of taking action.

Costs of Development

Last on the list of major benefits or costs influenced by zoning, but perhaps most important in distributive effect, are the costs of residential, commercial, or industrial development. This discussion will focus on the costs of housing, specifically on those cost increases which disproportionately fall on particular groups.

Restrictive techniques may cause the cost of certain types of housing to increase, thus excluding certain groups. The most notable of these techniques include

> (a) controls over density which raise the price of land per dwelling unit (e.g., minimum lot sizes); (b) minimum floor area requirements that compel the construction of larger houses than may be necessary for health reasons; (c) requirements for accessories such as garages, irrespective of market requirements; (d) architectural controls adopted in the name of aesthetics; and, (e) administrative delays and redundancies that add time and, hence, increase capital costs (Babcock and Bosselman 1973, p. 17).

Other, less notable techniques include exclusion of particular types of housing, e.g., apartments, townhouses, mobile homes, and "overzoning" of land for low-density residential, commercial, and industrial use. The rationale for each technique often varies with the location and the technique. Since all are exercises of the police power, their explicit purpose must be "protecting and promoting public health, safety, convenience, and general welfare." Their implicit purpose might be quite different. One often cited argument for restrictive techniques relates to the concept of "exclusionary" or "fiscal" zoning.[21]

Suburban communities contend that to curb demands upon public

21. Exclusionary here refers to zoning controls which interfere with the availability of housing affordable by low- and middle-income groups. For a detailed explanation, see Sagalyn and Sternlieb (1973, pp. 1–19), Babcock and Bosselman (1973, pp. 1–38), and Bergman (1974, Chapters 1–6).

services, e.g., education, police, fire protection, it is necessary to attract uses that produce net tax receipts or at least to exclude consumers of significantly larger than average amounts of these services. These communities fear that higher-density housing, which may attract low- and middle-income households, would precipitate a decline in per-capita property valuation. "Given the present state–local distribution of school costs, if such a decline occurred, tax rates would have to increase to sustain the community's present expenditure pattern for public services" (Sagalyn and Sternlieb 1973, p. 4). The avoidance of these presumed increased costs and maintenance of the status quo are often used to justify efforts to protect property values. Uses favored under exclusionary or fiscal zoning include light industry, research and development firms, and, to a lesser degree, low-density, high-value, single-family homes. In contrast, those not favored include multiple-family units, mobile homes, and high-density homes.

The most frequently attacked restrictive or exclusionary technique is probably "large lot" zoning. Both specific and general pressures on housing prices may result from mandatory lot sizes larger than the unregulated market would determine. Specific pressure may stem from the higher than average valuations of land and structures associated with large lot sizes. The fiscal rationale depends upon this assumption, but available evidence does not strongly support it.[22] General pressure results when "large lot" zoning ultimately restricts the supply of land available for residential use and thus raises the raw land component of housing costs. If this general pressure is significant, the price of all types of residential land will increase and raise the threshold of income classes excluded from single-family housing. Quantitative evidence of this pressure is scarce. Sagalyn and Sternlieb (1973, p. 11) state that raw land prices are significantly affected by both the number of different density districts in the municipality and the extent of district mapping but can offer no evidence for their assertion.

As reported earlier, Sagalyn and Sternlieb (1973) indicated that although a change in zoning policies making land available for higher-density, single-family units would not of itself generate housing for low- and moderate-income families, changes in restrictive practices with concomitant reductions in size and amenities by builders, would considerably enlarge the effective market. Bergman (1974) concluded

22. A 1958 Urban Land Institute Study indicated greater variation of housing valuation within lot size categories than between categories. Coke and Liebman (1961) found a .50 simple correlation between lot size and housing price and therefore concluded that large-lot zoning alone would not be an effective device for attracting higher-priced housing. Sagalyn and Sternlieb (1973, p. 66) found a .61 correlation and concurred with Coke and Liebman's conclusion.

that although the degree varied over townships, exclusion due to zoning requirements affected primarily, and often only, the lowest-income households. Many would retort that in a sense all prices are exclusionary since there are almost always some who cannot afford them. However, the important point is that the price of single-family housing for lower-income groups may increase in greater proportion than it does for middle- or high-income groups.

Other Benefits and Costs
Undoubtedly, zoning regulations generate other distributive effects. Discouraging the location of heavy industry may limit the availability of certain jobs in a local labor market. Reduction of competition in the real estate and building industries may result in higher rental and ownership costs. It is unfortunate that there is no relevant quantitative information relating to these potential effects.

Summary of Distributive Effects
The nature and occurrence of the distributive effects stemming from zoning are quite varied. The most important general effect is the potential for adding to the costs of housing, especially of units within the means of lower-income groups. Babcock and Bosselman (1973, p. 17) note that although the added cost attributable to each restrictive technique may be nominal, when combined, they may add substantially to housing costs.

The specific effects from attempting to reduce externalities, provide public goods, and lower the cost of public services appear to fall heavily on landowners. Those whose lands are zoned for higher-intensity use receive windfall gains, while those whose lands are designated for low intensity use suffer losses or wipeouts. To acquire specific benefits or avoid specific costs, transaction costs are usually incurred. For example, obtaining a favorable zoning decision usually requires substantial personal time, resources, and, perhaps, professional assistance. Assuming the transaction costs of obtaining windfalls or avoiding wipeouts are roughly equivalent for all parties, the price is less dear for landowners with high incomes or wealth or with larger or more valuable plots of land.

As a concluding note on zoning's distributive effects, the temporary nature of some zoning regulations deserves attention. The impermanence of zoning regulations has drawn criticism from many commentators who accused regulators of bending to economic incentives by granting variances, special exemptions, rezonings, and planned unit developments. Short-run changes in use intensity for a property may cause windfalls or wipeouts in terms of asset value, but these may be mitigated by further changes in zoning regulations. Theoretically, the value of land is the present value of all expected returns minus all expected costs from employing the land in its most intensive allowable use. Therefore, windfalls and wipeouts caused by zoning may be transitory, but regardless of their transitory nature, short-term zoning regulations may affect asset values and therefore permanently effect the wealth of certain real estate owners.

POLITICAL ASPECTS OF EXPANDING THE ROLE OF ZONING

Most political activity surrounding zoning occurs at the local level where zoning regulations are planned, administered, and changed. Some observers characterize changes in zoning ordinances as crucial to land use politics in the suburbs and, therefore, the base of suburban politics in general (Linowes and Allensworth 1973, pp. 59, 60). The conflict surrounding zone changes usually pits two traditional coalitions against each other.

The first coalition comprises developers, land speculators, builders, savings and loan associations, and allied groups who want to maintain control over land use planning (Godwin and Shepard 1975, pp. 14, 15). This coalition might be termed the *development group* and can be characterized as those who, responding to development market needs, also desire the highest private economic return from land development. The second coalition, termed the *neighborhood group*, usually comprises suburban residents who organize to fight off the introduction of "incompatible" uses into their neighborhood. Their expressed purpose is usually preserving the character of their neighborhood environment, which means excluding any land use they consider "undesirable". Both of these groups possess extensive political influence and therefore can punish elected land use decision-makers if development profits or home values are eroded.

Members of both groups are typically from middle to upper socioeconomic groups. Chapter 4 discussed the reasons for this. Lower-income groups are often heterogeneous, have little organizational experience, are not politically active, and have fewer resources to expend for effective organization. For these reasons, zoning usually becomes a middle and upper class matter. In consequence, regardless of the relatively open access to the political decision-making process afforded by the various hearings required by the procedure for zoning change, the participants (the upper income groups) do not usually emphasize the provision of housing within the means of the nonparticipants (lower income groups). In fact, most neighborhood groups organize to fight proposed land use changes that would make this type of housing available.

The expansion of zoning to encompass broader objectives such as the preservation of "prime" agriculatural land, open space, and critical environmental areas may shift the focus of conflict to a community's comprehensive land use plan and introduce new political participants. Since zoning regulations are a means of direct regulation under the police power, resources will be extracted from some groups and redistributed to others, and the potential winners and losers will be quite aware of the consequences. In these situations, political decision-makers who support proposed policies are visible to those who stand to lose, and they are likely to use these policies only when the demand for them is strong and well organized.

Providing open space areas on the fringe of a city illustrates the issues well. If the city utilizes zoning to preserve open space, landowners in the open space zone will lose any potential development value and receive no compensation. It is also probable that housing near the open space areas will increase in value because of the certainty of open spaces nearby. Although the phenomenon is not as visible, if the preservation of open space significantly reduces the amount of developable land and potential housing, the owners of such land will enjoy an increase in land values while buyers will face higher costs. The most visible effect, though, is to take the right to develop from some landowners and grant the right to enjoy open space to others.

Simply stated, the political acceptability of expanding the role of zoning in this manner will depend upon the relative political strength of groups expecting to gain or lose. As discussed in Chapter 4, salience of the issue, certainty of the outcomes, and clarity of the benefactors will all affect acceptability. Salience serves to define the interest groups and the degree to which they will participate. Potential interest by the traditional development and neighborhood groups is difficult to predict. If the landowners who stand to lose development value are part of the development coalition, then they may oppose such an expansion of zoning controls. If many neighborhood groups expect increased property values, they may support it. Probably the most support will come from environmental interest groups. They view public goods such as open space and critical environmental areas as fundamental policy goals. Whether they can effectively organize and exert significant political pressure at the local level is the question. Given the high rates of political participation of many of the potential losers in expanded zoning, such expansion will tend to be more politically acceptable only if it guarantees them compensation.

Whether an expansion in zoning will be politically acceptable in the absence of guaranteed compensation will depend on the ability of neighborhood and environmental groups to join forces. Since both are concerned with the quality of their living environment, such a coalition may be possible. Neighborhood groups may view the provision of open space as a way to isolate their residences from "incompatible" uses while enjoying increased property values, and environmentalists may receive increased value from the public goods without paying their share of the costs. When landowners restricted by open space zoning are not part of the development coalition, they stand little chance of negating the joined group's support. In general, the political acceptability of expanding the role of zoning from its traditional focus on external effects will depend upon many specifics: the spatial incidence of land use policies considered, the nature of the political structure in the jurisdiction, and the level at which the political conflict is engendered.

SUMMARY AND IMPLICATIONS

The primary rationale for both past and present application of zoning regulations centers on the control of "undesirable" external effects that arise from the juxtaposition of "incompatible" land uses. Many observations and objective measurements attest to the existence of these external effects, but even though many land uses may be subject to harmful external effects, it does not follow that zoning regulations have controlled or are capable of controlling these negative influences effectively. There are two reasons for this: first, reliance on separation of "incompatible" land uses and a host of regulations for each land use district are at best indirect techniques for controlling air quality, water pollution, noise levels, traffic congestion, and visual disamenities. Perhaps, techniques such as performance standards, which more directly identify the "offensive" characteristics would provide increasingly effective control. Second, despite planning efforts to specify potential external effects accurately and incorporate them into zoning ordinances, private economic incentives from the spatial location of land uses may attack and undermine comprehensive land use plans. Introduction of taxation and subsidy measures that address the external effects more directly may provide control more effectively than reliance on the spatial designation of land uses.

From an efficiency standpoint, a complete evaluation of zoning must include realized and potential benefits and costs other than those of eliminating external effects. Given an average cost pricing scheme, zoning regulations have the potential to reduce the costs of various public services by increasing development density and contiguity. However, zoning regulations that have actually decreased density and contiguity, e.g., minimum lot sizes, may have increased public service provision costs. Decreased development density and the segregation of residential, work, and shopping areas may also raise travel costs to a level higher than that desired by a community in the absence of zoning. The transaction costs of planning, implementing, changing, and enforcing a zoning ordinance appear to be significant, especially those of changing the ordinance. Some evidence indicates that zoning may increase the costs of development, particularly of certain types of housing, e.g., multiple-family, but this may not be a significant factor considering all other influences. Other potential benefits and costs include the longer horizons for those planning real estate investment assured by greater certainty of land use patterns and the reduction of competition in the real estate market. Considering the scant evidence relating to these benefits and costs and the prospect of increased public control of land use through zoning, serious further study seems warranted.

The social desirability of zoning is also contingent on its distribution of benefits and costs. In Stull's words:

> If, on the other hand, one is sure that zoning ordinances do significantly constrain the locational choices of households and firms, one may still wish to restrict the power of municipalities to zone because this power is so often used to exclude minority group members and persons with low income from neighborhoods and communities where they might otherwise be able to reside (1975, p. 553).

Middle and upper class communities often attempt to justify the exclusion of minority or low-income groups on the grounds that their inclusion would seriously erode the tax base and place excessive demand on public services. Nevertheless, given the hypothesis that higher-income groups also enjoy a greater proportion of zoning's specific benefits (windfalls), public policy decision-makers should seriously analyze its distributive consequences. "The concern with exclusionary land use controls is that almost all communities will exclude the same groups, those that are excluded from many other things in society" (Mills 1976, p. 57).

The contemplated expansion of zoning controls to provide such public goods as open space deserves serious thought before adoption. Because direct regulation measures like zoning make no attempt to assess the beneficiaries and compensate the losers, one would expect to find an oversupply of these public goods. Looking at the distribution of benefits and costs from other zoning efforts, one also expects that the potential beneficiaries will be higher-income groups while a more than proportionate share of costs falls on low-income groups. An expanded role for zoning will probably be politically feasible only if neighborhood and environmental groups form coalitions to counteract the opposition of landowners who stand to lose development value. Other techniques that attempt to collect some of the benefits and pay some of the costs should dampen the demand for these goods while mitigating some of the "undesirable" distributive effects. The next chapter will discuss zoning by eminent domain, a recently proposed technique for that purpose.

※ *Chapter 6*

Zoning by Eminent Domain

Today we are witnessing increased public control over what were once considered private land use perogatives (Bosselman and Callies 1971). In spite of a continuing belief by many that private property owners can do what they please with their land, recent rulings in state courts have tended to support the increasing public regulation of private property rights in land.[1] If increasing the scope of land use control is to be accomplished through zoning regulations, the incidence of specific distributive effects—windfalls and wipeouts—is likely to increase in both amount and severity. Although zoning is not the only land use control technique, it is undoubtedly the most pervasive. According to Bosselman, Callies, and Banta (1973), resort to the courts under the Fifth Amendment of the United States Constitution—". . . nor shall private property be taken for public purpose without just compensation"—will not provide relief. However, if those negatively affected are politically influential, the effective constraint on increasing public control of land use may be political rather than legal. At least partial compensation for the loss of valuable property rights may be necessary to make land use control more politically acceptable.

Many professionals associated with land use planning believe that unless windfall and wipeout problems are treated, any land use plan-

1. Courts have generally looked to Justice Holmes' balancing principle in this regard. Briefly summarized, it states that a "taking" does not occur if the public benefits outweigh the private costs to landowners. Obviously, a strict efficiency interpretation of this principle does not treat the equity implications of who receives the public benefits and who pays the private costs.

ning system will fall short of its objectives (Hagman 1975, pp. 278–281). Various techniques have been proposed or employed for addressing windfalls or wipeouts separately (Lowenberg et al. 1974). Recently, more attention has focused on techniques that combine windfall recapture and wipeout compensation. Two techniques proposed specifically for this purpose are transferable development rights (TDRs) and zoning by eminent domain (ZED).

This chapter will analyze the ZED concept and Chapter 6 will address the TDR system.[2] An outline of the hypothetical structure and operation of the ZED system will be presented in the first section, while the second reviews some actual applications of ZED to identify potential advantages and problems. Some issues critical to the successful operation of ZED are explored in the third section. Expected changes in zoning benefits and costs and their distribution will then be assessed followed by some aspects of the political acceptability of ZED.

STRUCTURE AND OPERATION OF A ZED SYSTEM

ZED is a modification of traditional zoning regulations specifically designed to treat windfall and wipeout problems (Hagman 1974, 1975). The idea originated around the turn of the century when it was unclear whether the courts would sanction zoning by police power. Briefly, the ZED system operates as follows. Assume that a city or other area is to be zoned. Following usual procedures, the responsible authority designates different areas for residential, commercial, and industrial purposes—the traditional separation of "incompatible" uses. To guard against wipeouts, however, eminent domain procedures are employed. The zoning authority acquires the development rights for all purposes other than those permitted under the zoning plan, and landowners are compensated to the extent that the taking of these rights lowered their

2. The zoning by eminent domain concept analyzed in this chapter is based on the recapture and compensation scheme developed by Donald Hagman which he terms zoning by special assessment financed eminent domain (ZSAFED). Since Hagman has been the primary figure in developing the ZED concept, the first section, on the structure and operation of a ZED system, draws heavily from his published work in this area (1974, 1975). For the section of the history of ZED applications and the remainder of the chapter, we have also had the benefit of reviewing a draft article by Hagman on ZED entitled "Zoning by Special Assessment Financed Eminent Domain (ZSAFED)," appearing in *University of Florida Law Review*, 28, (in press) and in *Windfalls for Wipeouts* (D. Hagman and D. Misczynski, American Society of Planning Officials, forthcoming), hereafter referred to as Hagman 1976. This chapter attempts to apply the efficiency, distributive effects, and political acceptability analyses of Chapters 2, 3, and 4 to the zoning by eminent domain concept. The reader is referred to Hagman's work for a full discussion of the structure, history, and operational particulars of his ZSAFED concept.

property values.[3] Because wipeouts are only one side of the coin, the windfall feature is employed. The distribution of property values is shifted into accord with the distribution of land use intensities defined by the zoning plan. Consequently, some property becomes more valuable. This property is specially assessed to recapture the increment resulting from public action. In other words, those properties permitted more intensive development must pay for the associated development rights. Thus, it may be possible to finance wipeout payments by collecting windfalls.

A comparison of the ZED and TDR techniques reveals similarities and differences. The essence of the TDR system is also separating the rights to develop property so that property owners whose land is restricted from potential use can sell their development rights to those whose property is zoned for higher intensities. Since those wishing to develop to a higher intensity are required to purchase development rights in addition to land, there is a quasi-private market which, in concept, compensates wipeouts and recaptures windfalls. TDRs and ZED can be viewed as alternative ways of implementing the same land use plan. Both trade windfalls for wipeouts.

But there are some significant differences, mostly in the incidence and amount of wipeout compensation and windfall recapture. A system of TDRs would establish a publicly administered market for the private transfer of development rights. That is, it would distribute development rights to landowners whose property had been restricted from potential development on the basis of changes in land values from before regulation to after, but owners of land designated for increased intensity would be required to buy some of these development rights before they could begin to develop their land. In general, the value of each development right would depend on the number of rights distributed, the amount of property designated for increased intensity, the land and housing markets, and the natural development pressure in the zoning jurisdiction.

In contrast, ZED entails the public purchase and sale of development rights. Therefore, the magnitude and occurrence of wipeout compensation and windfall recapture under ZED would be determined by publicly estimated land values before and after the impostition of zoning controls. Although both ZED and TDR rely, to a degree, upon public administration, the distribution of wipeout compensation and windfall recapture would probably vary between systems. The nature

3. Hagman's conception of the ZED technique (1976), views wipeout compensation as payment of damages rather than the public purchase of restricted development rights. The following discussion retains the latter interpretation, but the damage payment view should not significantly alter the results of this analysis.

of the variation is impossible to determine until ZED and TDRs have been tried on a wide scale, but, in general, it will depend on specific rules and administrative details.

ZED APPLICATIONS

A brief capsulization of applications of the concept of zoning by eminent domain may help to provide a guide for identifying potential problems and advantages.[4]

Probably the widest application of ZED occurred in Minnesota before the passage of a comprehensive zoning enabling act, when a residential district act based on the power of eminent domain was passed by the state legislature in 1915. In practice, the act resembled a publicly regulated system of restrictive covenants in residential areas with compensation for those who sustained losses. Under the act, a petition from 50% of the land-owners in a district authorized the city council to designate and establish "restricted residence districts." Certain buildings were forbidden in these districts, but restricted landowners received compensation for loss of potential use value and owners whose land values increased were specially assessed to recapture the additional increment. City-appointed appraisers made the initial determination of benefits and damages and the city council made final confirmation. Any appeal of unfair determinations was settled by court-appointed appraisers. Total benefits assessed were limited to total damages plus assessment costs, and interest was paid on delayed damage payments. The Minnesota Supreme Court ruled the act constitutional in *State ex. rel. Twin City Building and Investment Co. vs. Houghton, 144 Minn* (1919, 1920). The state legislature allowed cities to float bonds secured by the special assessments to pay damages and permitted annual installments for benefit payments. In 1923 the original legislation was amended so that a city council could eliminate restrictions for a district if 50% of the landowners so petitioned, again with damages and benefits assessed for the change.

Although restricted residential districts can be found in Minnesota today, support for zoning under police power relegated ZED to a relatively minor role. Anderson (1927) indicated three major shortcomings in the Minnesota system, including (1) the cost of condemning restricted properties and identifying, measuring, and determining property value adjustments, (2) the possibility that property owners in restricted districts would falsely announce development intentions and thereby

---

4. This description of applications is taken from the forthcoming article by Hagman (1976) referred to in note 2 and Lowenberg et al. (1974). The reader is referred to these sources for a fuller and more detailed discussion.

receive damages, and (3) the inflexibility of land use patterns in a district once restrictions were applied.

A more limited application of the ZED concept occurred in Kansas City in 1893. Under city charter and ordinance powers, an exclusively residential district could be formed restricting business uses, but only for a maximum of 20 years. In other characteristics the system closely resembled that of Minnesota. In a 1969 court test (*City of Kansas City vs. Kindle* [Mo.] 1969) the ordinance was found to be a joint exercise of the police and eminent domain powers since it was implemented for a public purpose and bore a substantial relation to the public health, safety, morals, or general welfare.

Aside from a short-lived 1917 application in a small Wisconsin village, these two cases are the only ZED experiments. Nevertheless, in both the legality of zoning by eminent domain was upheld. Broadening ZED to encompass such land use objectives as providing open space or preserving prime agricultural land will surely elicit much legal argument. However, before approaching that stage, the above discussion of ZED's structure, operation, and history point to some important general issues which deserve examination.

GENERAL ISSUES

The ability of a system of zoning by eminent domain to achieve its objectives will depend on a number of potential problem areas, including

1. identification of windfalls and wipeouts,
2. measurement of changes in value of affected land,
3. financial solvency, and
4. other specific characteristics.

Each of these subjects will be discussed in turn.[5]

Identification of Windfalls and Wipeouts

If windfalls and wipeouts are defined as changes in land values due to zoning regulations, then other land value changes due to individual or private market actions can be ignored.[6] This is much easier said

5. For a good general discussion of these potential issues and other problems surrounding compensatory land use regulations see Bureau of Governmental Research and Service (1975).

6. Hagman (1976) suggests that as zoning is replaced with new systems of land use control, the recapture and compensation of benefits and damages due to these new techniques should also fall under his ZSAFED system.

than done. As explained in Chapter 5, the value of a piece of land is affected by two sets of factors. First comprises those specific to the site such as location, physical characteristics, public services, and zoning classification. The second set is comprised of general factors that may affect all land values in a jurisdiction—population and economic growth rates, the extent to which zoning regulations restrict the effective supply of developable land, and property tax rates. As these factors vary among land parcels or change over time, the value of a piece of land will be affected.

Since expectations about net returns from buying or selling it determine the value of a tract of land, changes in zoning regulations applicable to it (or to nearby land for that matter) can exert a positive or a negative influence. Rose (1971) showed that some farmland may have a "capital value" based on capitalized net returns expected from farming, a higher "development value" derived from expectations about the capitalized value from urban uses, and a "market value" lying at some level between the other two and reflecting the probability of rezoning and the provision of public services. The market and development values should be close if the probability of rezoning and public service provision is high but if the probability is low, the market value should approach the capital value. Under a ZED system, if land is zoned for exclusively agricultural use, the owner would receive partial or full compensation for any loss in value.

Implementation of a ZED system will require a structured procedure for identifying windfalls and wipeouts due to zoning regulations that incorporates several basic principles. Zoning changes can produce two types of effects. First, changes may affect the use intensity of a parcel of land, i.e., a direct effect. Rezoning residential land from single-family to high-density, multiple-family housing is an example. Increasing use intensity will increase land values if the development market needs land at the increased intensity. By the same token, decreasing the use intensity may decrease values.

The second type of effect occurs when the value of some land is affected by changes in the zoning regulations applicable to other land, i.e., indirect effects. Examples abound in any urban setting. Locating a service station next to a neighborhood of single-family homes will probably lower at least some property values. Preserving a farmer's prime agricultural land may not only lower his property values but also increase the value of adjacent residential property. Restricting the supply of developable land in a zoning jurisdiction may cause the value of developed land to rise above the level that the unregulated market would set.

Responsibility for identifying these direct and indirect effects will probably fall on the property tax assessment system (Hagman 1974, 1976). Minnesota's ZED experience with specially appointed appraisers led to high administrative costs which kept the system from spreading. In some states statutes currently require that assessors be notified of all zoning changes. This procedure covers direct effects but does not help to identify indirect effects. One expects that land owners experiencing decreased values would assist assessors to identify them as indirect effects but that those receiving windfalls might not readily volunteer this information. In general, then, we may infer that first: direct effects will be easier to identify than indirect effects; and second: those suffering losses will assist in identification but those experiencing gains will not—which implies that assessors' time and resources will be spent most heavily in identifying indirect windfalls. It is difficult to predict what percentage of total windfalls come from indirect effects. Holding rigidly to the complete windfall identification and special assessment proceedings that would be necessary to compensate for all associated wipeouts might prove too costly. Broader financing measures such as property taxes might be necessary to capture a portion of the indirect windfalls, especially for zoning actions that generate wide benefits, e.g., preservation of critical environmental areas.

Measurement of Changes in Value of Affected Land

Once the affected properties have been identified, the increments and decrements in value attributable only to the zoning action must be measured, a process that will be beset by many problems. Errors in assessment will redistribute wealth, but probably not in the desired way, and may have undesirable effects on land-market allocations. With any ZED system, correct measurements will necessitate establishing the value of affected properties immediately before and immediately after a zone change, apart from other land-market influences. Realistically, assessment will require some period of time, the length of which will depend upon the resources available to the assessment system, but if the assessments before and after a zoning change are not performed within a short period, account will have to be taken of other factors that may also have influenced land values during the interval.

Figure 6.1 illustrates some of the potential problems in simple form. Assume the landowner was employing the land in use B until the zone change at time T_1. Assume also that the market value of the land is B_1 in use B at T_1 and entered on the tax assessment roles accordingly. If the zoning action at T_1 restricts the land to use A, the market

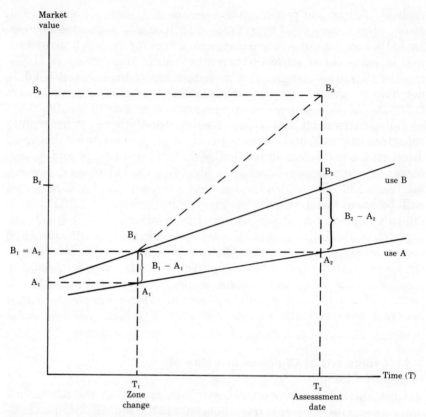

Figure 6.1. Potential measurement problems with land value changes over time.

value drops to A_1 and the landowner experiences a decline in wealth of $B_1 - A_1$. However, if compensation is computed by comparing B_1, the assessed value before the zoning change in use B, with A_2, the assessed value after the zoning change to use A, no loss of value is indicated. Obviously, under full compensation provisions, the landowner should receive $B_1 - A_1$ at T_1 or $B_2 - A_2$ at T_2. Failure to account for the factors which cause the price of land to rise over time, such as the real rate of return on land in uses A and B and the declining value of the dollar (i.e., inflation), can cause problems.

Let us reverse the initial conditions and assume that the landowner was employing the land in use A at T_1 and the zone change allowed a shift to use B. Assuming the same measurement procedure as above, how does the time lag in assessment affect the calculations of windfall recapture? Under these assumptions, the assessed value before the change, A_1, is compared to the assessed value after the change, B_2. Under full recapture provisions, the landowner would be assessed $B_2 - A_1$ when the true windfall is $B_1 - A_1$ at T_1 or $B_2 - A_2$ at T_2. Therefore, in cases where land values are rising for both uses, the time lag in assessment will understate wipeout compensation and overstate windfall recapture. Both affected parties would be unhappy.

The problem lies in comparing assessed values at two different times without accounting for the factors which cause land prices to change over time. What about the alternative of making both assessments at T_2? This will provide a reliable guide only when the value of land between T_1 and T_2 is not affected by any factors except the average real rate of return on land investment and inflation. For example, if, as in the first case, the landowner is restricted to use A from use B at time T_1, and the market value of the land in use B shifts abruptly upward to B_3 at T_2, assessment of both uses at T_2 results in $B_3 - A_2$ per acre, and may overstate the "desired" level of wipeout compensation. As discussed in Chapter 5, many exogenous factors can affect the return or market value of different types of land in the short run. If the measurement system is faced with a considerable time lag in determining the increments and decrements in value caused by zoning action, account will have to be taken of these factors along with inflation and normal rates of return foregone.

Even if nearly immediate assessment is feasible, the values of affected land before and after a zone change may prove a faulty guide. Land subject to potential zone changes, especially on the fringe of conversion areas, will often change value rapidly and substantially prior to any formal public action (Alonzo 1964, p. 51). Buyers and sellers estimate the probability of public actions such as changes in zoning and the provision of public services and make their bids and offers accordingly. Therefore, basing wipeout compensation on land values immediately preceding and following a zone change may still transfer the value of public action to private landowners.

Apart from the problems inherent in the process itself, a measurement system must be provided. Hagman (1974, 1976) suggests that our current property tax assessment system has the framework required for implementing a ZED system. Some states are close to operating systems where property taxes are based on computerized models of property values. Of course, any model requires data reflecting the specific regional and local characteristics of the land market and is only as sound as the design of the underlying estimation procedure. In many cases implementing a ZED system will require increased assessment frequency and accuracy. Carefully designed computer systems could undoubtedly aid in this effort. Both increases would probably require additional resources for the tax assessment system.

Financial Solvency

At first glance, it may seem obvious that a ZED system would have no problems in sustaining itself financially. In fact, if zoning does its job well, the benefits assessed under a ZED system should outweigh the losses compensated (Hagman 1976) since many contend that good planning should result in increased total land value for the planning area. However, several issues require closer scrutiny before this view can be accepted. These issues fall into two broad categories. First, *assuming* that windfalls and wipeouts are identified, measured, and recaptured with equal accuracy and at the same rate (partial or full), the financial solvency of a ZED system will depend on whether or not windfalls actually offset wipeouts plus transaction costs (ignoring problems of recapture and compensation timing). Second, one must question the assumption that all land value changes caused by zoning will be identified, measured, and collected with equal accuracy. Each of these issues will be addressed in turn.

As described in Chapter 5, zoning regulations can cause a variety of benefits and costs. Not only may land values be affected, but the costs of structures may be separately influenced through restrictions on the supply allowed of certain types of housing, e.g., multiple family, and on certain housing characteristics, e.g., minimum floor area. In general, ZED concerns itself largely with the recapture and compensation of land value changes.

Conceptually, at least, zoning can increase or decrease the value of a jurisdiction's land base and also shift value among land parcels. The latter effect is derived from the nature of zoning regulations to determine the spatial distribution of land use intensities. Moving a highly desired commercial zone to a multiple-family housing area will probably increase the value of the newly zoned land and decrease the value of property that lost the commercial zoning. If this were the sole effect of zoning regulations, a ZED system would have a relatively uncomplicated task.

Because they can change the overall supply of and/or demand for land, zoning regulations are also capable of increasing or decreasing the total value of land in a jurisdiction. When total windfalls exceed total wipeouts, an increase in total land value will result, and vice versa. The traditional rationale for zoning, eliminating external effects, is (or should be) based on the ability of zoning to increase the intrinsic desirability, i.e., demand, of land for all purposes by separating "incompatible" uses. Figure 6.2 illustrates some effects from demand changes. Assume the supply of land for development (S) is fixed in the short run at $S_0 S_0$. If the demand for land shifts from $D_0 D_0$ to $D_1 D_1$ because of zoning regulations obviously an increase in the total value of the quantity S_0 of land results. The opposite effect, lessening the desirability of land (i.e., moving from $D_1 D_1$ to $D_0 D_0$), yields a decrease in total value. This might occur where minimum parcel or lot sizes are so restrictive that they increase the cost of housing to a point where the demand for residential land is actually reduced.

Zoning regulations can also influence the supply of land for development (Figure 6.3). Assume that the short-run supply of development land is restricted from $S_0 S_0$ to $S_1 S_1$ when zoning regulations place effective limitations on land available for development. The market value of land before the new restrictions is represented by the rectangle $OP_0 E S_0$. The effect on the total value of land in the jurisdiction will depend upon the shape of the demand curve as illustrated by

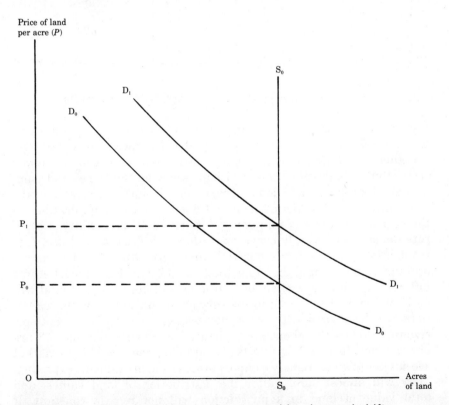

Figure 6.2. Changes in land value caused by demand shifts.

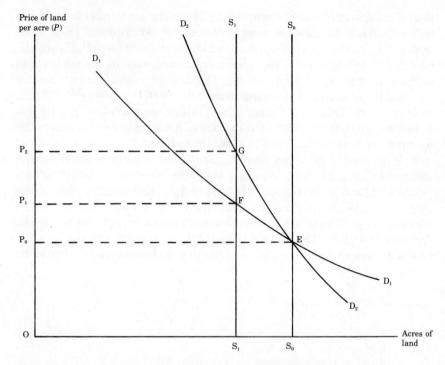

Figure 6.3. Changes in land value caused by supply shifts.

the alternative curves D_1D_1 and D_2D_2. With D_1D_1, the total value becomes OP_1FS_1 while with D_2D_2 total value increases to OP_2GS_1. Whether total land value increases or decreases because of the supply restriction is impossible to tell without knowing the slopes and magnitudes of the supply and demand curves for the jurisdiction analyzed.

Admittedly, these discussions and diagrams are simplifications of the real-world effects of zoning regulations. In all probability, a separate demand and supply curve exists for each type of land use, e.g., residential, commercial, industrial, and agricultural, and a zoning ordinance and changes thereto is likely to affect each land market in a differential manner. The supply curve for different types of land will probably not be fixed, even in the very short run, since zoning regulations can be altered with many devices, e.g., variances, exceptions, rezonings. Thus the phenomena pictured in Figures 6.2 and 6.3 are abstractions. In short, the effects of zoning in a real-world land market are subject to an extremely complex process and are difficult to predict. They will almost surely alter the distribution of land values, and total value of land in a jurisdiction will not remain constant. If land use planning through zoning regulations is successful, i.e., increase total land value, total windfalls should offset total wipeouts, but this is by no means obvious; and even if windfalls exceed wipeouts, the transaction costs of operating a ZED system remain to be considered. The role of transaction costs will be discussed in more detail later in this chapter.

The second major issue relating to the financial solvency of a ZED system is the expected accuracy of identifying and measuring windfalls and wipeouts. The sections on identification and measurement above suggested that both direct and indirect changes in land values will stem from zoning actions. The direct effects will be easiest to identify and measure since they result from changes in use intensity. The indirect effects—a diverse set of potential changes in land values caused by the zoning regulation of other pieces of property in a jurisdiction—are, therefore, more difficult to identify and measure. Preventing the development of an apartment building by changing the zoning on the fringe of a district zoned for single-family residential use will decrease the value of the land formerly zoned for multiple family residences, i.e., a direct effect, while increasing the value of single-family lots which might otherwise have been negatively affected, i.e., indirect effects. The composite occurrence and degree (dollar value) of direct and indirect effects for a zoning jurisdiction depends on the nature of zoning actions employed. As explained above, those who suffer direct or indirect wipeouts can be expected to assist the assessor in identifying and measuring their losses, but those receiving direct or indirect windfalls will probably not offer assistance. Considering the easier identification of direct effects, indirect windfalls represent the greatest problem and, depending upon their relative importance, could hinder the financial solvency of a ZED system.

Other Specific Characteristics

When to Recapture and Compensate.   Some might argue that "immediate" wipeout compensation and windfall recapture are unnecessary since the affected parties will experience changes in wealth only when their land is sold.[7] Along these lines, a proposal similar to ZED (Institute for Environmental Studies 1968) suggested that compensation be paid only when the affected land is transferred. Under this type of proposal, an assessor would record the value of potentially affected property just before zoning action. If the property were trans-

---

7. In fact, if property tax effects are considered, landowners gaining value lose part of their wealth increase and those losing value will have lower property taxes. The deduction of property tax liabilities in computing federal taxable income would tend to dampen this effect.

ferred at a later date, the government would pay any loss or collect any gain in value based on the difference between sale value and assessed value, taking inflation into account. ZED proposals, on the other hand, usually provide for immediate recapture or compensation. What are the implications of redressing wealth changes only if or when the land is transferred?

The income of landowners who suffer losses would decline only if a zoning action decreases their returns from employing affected property in a use now prohibited, or to the extent that land at higher values was being used as collateral for loans (ignoring property and income tax effects). In either case, the landowner affected negatively would have an incentive to sell the land and receive wipeout compensation. The degree of incentive would of course depend on the proportion of his total wealth and/or income the wipeout constituted. In contrast, the income of landowners whose property values increase would rise only if the zoning action allowed an increased use intensity that yielded greater net returns or if the increased land value was used as collateral to secure a loan. The degree of incentive to hold the property affected positively would also depend on the proportion of wealth and/or income the windfall represents. To the extent that these conditions hold, the general incentive under the "transfer only" criterion would be for those experiencing losses to sell affected property and those benefiting to keep it.

The "transfer only" proposal does have some advantages over "immediate" recapture and compensation (Lowenberg et al. 1974, p. 114). First, since property must be sold to qualify for either compensation or recapture, a smaller administration and financing burden should be expected (unless all affected landowners should decide to transfer their property). Some of the assessment burden would also be relieved since assessment after zoning action would be performed by observing the market value of transferred property. Second, greater flexibility would be afforded since zoning regulations could be altered repeatedly for any affected property without requiring return of compensation already paid or reimbursement of collected windfalls.

The "transfer only" criterion is not without disadvantages. Its most serious problem would be accounting for factors other than the zoning action that influence the value of affected land between the date of a zoning change and the date of transfer. Figure 6.1 illustrated the inflationary forces that could hamper identification and measurement under immediate recapture and compensation provisions. Lengthening the time between the zoning action and land value adjustment could only result in more difficulty. In addition, complete reliance on transfer as a guide might miss some important windfalls and wipeouts. A landowner who enjoys the opportunity of increased use intensity could choose to develop his property himself, thereby receiving any potential windfall. For completeness and in the interests of fairness of application, i.e., procedural equity, the "transfer only" decision rule should be expanded to include compensation and recapture if affected properties are sold and/or change use after the zoning action.

Rate of Recapture and Compensation.   A most important issue for a ZED system is the rate at which compensation would be paid and windfalls collected. Some might suggest full adjustment for real losses or gains while others favor only partial compensation and recapture. Obviously, the degree is important in terms of the distribution of benefits and costs for zoning actions. To the extent that publicly caused losses or gains are not fully compensated or appropriated, the distribution of wealth will differ after a zoning change. If it is assumed that most land value adjustments will primarily affect landowners, then ZED can be viewed as a "within category" equity device; all landowners being the category of concern.

All previous applications of the ZED concept required full recapture of benefits (not to exceed total assessed damages) and full payment of damages. Hagman (1976) recommends a less than full rate of adjustment. His reasons are twofold. First, the inherent inadequacies of any assessment system, regardless of current computing technology, make partial adjustment more palatable. "Minor" changes in land values, perhaps a 10% to 20% minimum, would be ignored and a partial rate would be applied to changes exceeding the minimum. Second, full adjustment might eliminate most risk from the land market and thus inhibit change and progress. These are valid concerns, but any departure from a full adjustment rate would modify the distribution of wealth that existed prior to zoning action and therefore create an allocative equity issue. This issue might be more important if, as hypothesized in the discussion of political behavior in Chapter 4, the zoning system continued to distribute specific benefits to the more advantaged, i.e., higher socioeconomic classes, and specific costs to the less advantaged. However, given the present system of a zero rate of adjustment, any positive recapture or compensation rate could be considered an improvement.

Planning Inflexibility.   Any compensation and recapture scheme might restrict the flexibility of a governing body in planning (Bureau of Governmental Research 1974, pp. 20, 21). Once compensation and recapture were made for a zoning action, further alteration of the comprehensive plan might reverse the initial effects. Under the ZED concept, previous compensation payments and recapture assessments could be reversed if the original development rights were reestablished. The need to carry out time-consuming compensation and recapture for every alteration in zoning plans would encumber the flexibility of police power zoning. If one ponders the many changes in the comprehensive plan and zoning ordinances taking place in any one community over a one-year period, this problem takes on significance.

Corruption. ZED advocates cite windfall recapture and wipeout compensation as deterents to such current abuses as bribery which may characterize the zoning process (Hagman 1974, p. 114). The potential benefits of securing a favorable zoning decision have often proved to be an ample incentive to influence public officials illegally. Would ZED really change the present problem? Similar incentives could arise to influence the process of identifying and measuring windfalls and wipeouts.

Level of Administration. Although ZED was authorized by statute in Minnesota, application was left to individual cities. Comprehensive statewide ZED implementation may be the only workable approach, because differential land use activity can occur between smaller jurisdictions. If ZED does in fact reduce risk in the land market, speculative activity could increasingly shift to areas without ZED coverage.

We have traditionally thought of zoning power as the province only of local governments, but recent land use control activity has included state governments. Oregon's Land Conservation and Development Commission has issued land use goals and guidelines that cities and counties must incorporate into their comprehensive plans, and resulting zoning changes might not have occurred without this impetus. Where local land use costs generate benefits applicable more to the state than to the locality, the question of state-level administrative and financial support deserves consideration. The preservation of "prime" agricultural land may be an appropriate example.

The preceding discussion of general issues, although by no means complete, touches on some problem areas that may complicate or hinder ZED's success. Actual implementation of a ZED system will surely generate more operational problems.

BENEFITS AND COSTS OF ZED

Since there have been few ZED applications, what follows is largely a hypothetical analysis of potential effects. Yet, even this exercise can be useful to public land use decision-makers evaluating ZED's potential for land use control. Since ZED is viewed as a modification of traditional zoning regulations, the framework utilized to evaluate potential benefits and costs is similar to that employed in Chapter 5. While it is a less than complete enumeration of benefits and costs, this discussion identifies what are thought to be the major effects.

External Effects

Chapter 5 suggested that zoning's performance in eliminating external effects may be suspect on two counts. First, the separation of "incompatible" land uses is an indirect means of controlling external effects such as water pollution, noise levels, and esthetic disamenities. A ZED system would not directly alter this problem.[8] Second, and most important for the present discussion, the resistance of zoning regulations to individual and interest-group pressures for change has not been uniform among different land uses and different jurisdictions. By establishing varying use intensity districts, those owning low-intensity land have an incentive to secure rezoning to a higher intensity if the expected benefits outweigh the expected costs. Clawson (1971, p. 76) observed that the probability of achieving such rezoning depends in general on the type of neighborhood. Higher income single-family residential areas can usually unite and fight a zone change that would cause "perceived" negative external effects. Other newly formed or less homogeneous neighborhoods are often less capable of organizing.

Would a windfall recapture and wipeout compensation system like ZED help to reduce or eliminate incentives for plan breaking? If changes in land values caused by zoning actions could be identified, measured, and adjusted accurately, then, in concept at least, the incentive for plan breaking should be reduced (Hagman 1974, p. 116). A developer would know that any increase in land value achieved by obtaining a zoning change would be partially or fully recaptured. Lacking the prospect of large windfalls, landowners and developers should be less inclined to influence public officials illegally, but, as discussed above, corruption might manifest itself in the identification and measurement phases. That is, if a developer can obtain a lower windfall assessment "under the table," the rezoning may still be a profitable venture.

Assuming this illegal activity were not a pervasive influence, a

---

8. The possibility exists that zoning decision-makers could devote more time to specification and control of external effects if a ZED system significantly reduces requested zone changes, which currently predominate the zoning process (Hagman 1974, p. 115).

reduction in plan breaking might reduce the extent of external effects introduced by zone changes. Effectiveness in reducing significant negative external effects, however, still depends on accurate specification of those effects by the land use plan. ZED can only augment the strength of the zoning ordinances as drawn. If, as suggested in Chapter 5, zone changing indicates areas where potential efficiency gains can be realized, ZED might hinder efficiency improvements by reducing these changes.

Public Goods

Recent concern over such public goods as critical environmental areas has been responsible in part for the consideration of land use control techniques like TDR and ZED. Chapter 5 indicated that use of zoning, i.e., direct regulation, might be more inefficient than necessary in providing these public goods, since no mechanism explicitly weighs benefits and costs. The use of a ZED system represents a potential improvement for public goods provision.

As an example of how a ZED system might operate in providing a public good, suppose a city wishes to create an open space area adjacent to a rapidly expanding residential district. Assume that the land designated for open space is also suitable for development. Under normal zoning procedure, the land would be zoned for nondevelopment and the costs of this absorbed by the owners of the open space area while the benefits accrued to owners of adjacent land and others who might enjoy the open space.[9] If eminent domain proceedings or scenic easements were used, the restricted landowners would be compensated from general revenues, e.g., property taxes, for the loss of development rights. Under ZED, the procedure would vary from either of these alternatives. The land would still be zoned as open space, but owners of properties either positively or negatively affected would either (fully or partially) pay or be paid amounts in proportion to the increases or decreases in their property values. In essence, there would be an attempt to charge the beneficiaries and compensate the losers, at least to the extent that benefits and costs of the open space are reflected in changed property values.

The ZED mechanism is, therefore, a first approximation at balancing the incremental benefits and costs that stem from supplying certain public goods. The potential of direct regulation—zoning—for over-supplying land-related public goods is offset to a degree. The offsetting

9. If the open space area represents a considerable proportion of remaining residential land in the city, then the average price of residential land may rise granting a windfall to owners.

nature will depend, of course, on the accuracy with which affected property values are identified and measured and the rate of recapture and compensation. A complication to the ZED procedure is the fact that the benefits of some land-related public goods, such as preservation of critical environmental areas, may transcend local areas. ZED is not well equipped to handle such cases since special assessment of large, diverse groups is not possible. Wider sources of financial support, such as state and federal subsidies, could be justified to augment local assessments in these cases.

That ZED provides a first approximation and not an optimum method of providing public goods is partly a result of its lack of a mechanism for choosing the type and location of these goods. Administrators are expected to interpret citizen preferences. A mechanism for choosing public goods would require that those who are specially assessed or otherwise asked to pay for the public goods have the option of voicing their preferences.

Public Services

Development contiguity and density are influential determinants of public service costs. Land use planning can take them into account, but if a plan is continually "broken," costs may increase. For example, allowing increased housing density in an area where existing transportation networks, sewage pumping stations, and water lines are already utilized to capacity will require new facilities and investment. If ZED discourages "plan breaking," as contended, the efficiency of utilizing planned public service infrastructure may increase (Hagman 1974, p. 116).

Increased Certainty and Private Land Investments

The increased certainty of land use patterns may also encourage private land investments. That is, a landowner assured about the uses of neighboring land may undertake maintenance operations and capital investments reflecting a longer planning horizon. Agricultural land on the urban fringe is a good example. Many complain about the loss of agricultural production from land idle for a number of years before its conversion to urban uses. If fringe land were zoned for exclusively agricultural use under ZED, the landowner would be compensated for loss of development value and secure expectations about future agricultural use. With this increased certainty offered by a ZED system but not by traditional zoning regulations, the landowner would be more likely to undertake long-term capital investments, e.g., drainage, liming.

Transaction Costs

As discussed in Chapter 5, the transaction costs for a land use planning technique depend on the size of the adminstrative structure required and the manner in which responsibility for action is assigned. In analyzing zoning's transaction costs, we found it convenient to divide the process into four steps: planning; decision-making; amendments and change; and implementation. At first glance, the first and second steps should remain largely unaltered by a ZED system, but the last two should undergo considerable change. If ZED performs as contended, the number of requested zone changes should decrease substantially since the economic incentives for change will be reduced or eliminated by recapturing windfalls and compensating wipeouts. This would reduce transaction costs for the change phase.

Probably the greatest change in transaction costs will, however, occur in the implementation phase. With ZED this step must include the acts of identifying, measuring, and collecting or paying changes in land value due to zoning action. The property-tax assessment system would be likely to serve as a basis for performing the additional functions. Previous sections on identification and measurement suggested some of the problems in assessment that would have to be solved if a ZED system is to achieve its objectives. Increased assessment costs will cause the transaction costs for the implementation phase to increase under ZED; the degree will depend upon the accuracy of windfall recapture and wipeout compensation desired.

Development Costs

ZED in and of itself does not possess the potential to increase land or structure costs, but as a modification to zoning it may improve the ability of land use planning to achieve "desired" use patterns. If these "desired" patterns mean lower-intensity development—a reduction in developable land—the costs of development would increase, other factors held constant. This is a highly speculative argument, the strength of which will vary over zoning jurisdictions depending on their comprehensive land use plans.

DISTRIBUTIVE EFFECTS OF ZED

The primary objective of a ZED system is to fully or partially restore affected land values to their levels prior to a change in zoning. Of particular concern are adjustments to increases and decreases in the value of individual parcels of land attributable to zoning action, i.e., specific distributive effects. From a distributive perspective interest should center on the ultimate incidence of windfall assessments and wipeout compensation under ZED.

The analysis of specific distributive effects presented in Chapter 5 suggested that significant transaction costs are usually incurred when affected parties must take action to receive specific benefits or avoid specific costs of zoning regulations. Assuming these transaction costs are roughly equivalent for all landowners, it was hypothesized that the probability of receiving specific benefits or avoiding specific costs increases as income levels rise, other factors being constant. A ZED system is aimed directly at eliminating these specific distributive effects. Therefore, to the extent that windfalls and wipeouts are accurately identified, measured, and collected or dispersed, the distribution of landowner wealth prior to zoning action will be preserved afterwards under ZED. If our hypothesis about specific distributive effects is accurate, then the wealth position of lower-income landowners should improve under ZED relative to their position under zoning without recapture and compensation provisions. As explained earlier in this chapter, this is an allocative equity concern within the category of landowners. ZED does not directly address any of the allocative inequities that might occur between landowner and nonlandowner categories under police power zoning regulations.

Other, more general distributive effects may stem from ZED's influence on "plan breaking" and development sprawl. If lower levels of developable land and housing—or just significant lags in adjustment for the land and housing markets—are experienced, the average prices of land and housing may rise. However, these effects should not be attributed to a ZED system; they actually depend on the proper incorporation of land and housing "needs" into the comprehensive land use plan.

POLITICAL ACCEPTABILITY OF ZED

Since the ZED concept has not enjoyed widespread application, any assessment of its political palatability is necessarily tentative. Two prospects related to the introduction of a ZED system deserve attention. First, the underlying land use control objectives often associated with a windfall recapture and wipeout compensation scheme may help define interest groups. Second, specific characteristics of the ZED system itself may identify potential supporters and adversaries.

New land use control techniques such as TDR and ZED are being proposed, in large part, in response to the likely opposition to expanding the role of direct regulation, particularly zoning, to encompass broader land use planning objectives. Although the broad use of zoning has enjoyed favorable decisions from the courts, further expansion and, therefore, further restriction of private property rights in land may raise political obstacles.

If we assume that a ZED system would be most strongly associated with environmental goals such as preserving open-space areas its strongest support would come from the environmental coalition. The environmentalists' support may be tempered by their unfamiliarity with ZED's expected capability of achieving environmental policy goals. Over time, if provision of environmental goods through ZED imposes financial burdens on members of environmental groups, their continued support may wane, and renewed interest in traditional zoning may follow. Neighborhood groups may also envision the land use policies associated with ZED as ways to limit new development and protect the stability, quality, and value of their residential land, but they too may shy away if they experience heavy windfall assessments on their property.

Opposition to the land use policies associated with implementing a ZED system is more difficult to predict. Assuming losses in development value are fully compensated, the development interest group may not oppose it unless they view increasing quantities of land for open space and environmental areas as potential restrictions on development latitude. Buyers of new homes and renters may pay higher prices if the housing supply is reduced by preserving open space and environmental areas, but these groups are typically composed of recent inmigrants and young people who have yet to develop the political strength with which to block adoption of new land use controls.

A ZED system as proposed by Hagman (1974, 1975, 1976) pertains to all zoning actions and therefore encompasses all land use objectives pursued under the police power authority. Its major influence on more traditional objectives is to decrease the "plan breaking" associated with direct regulation. Depending on their expectations of realizing this increased certainty of land use patterns, the neighborhood groups and environmental interests may support ZED as a means of preserving the quality of residential living environments. The development group could be expected to oppose ZED if they have traditionally enjoyed large windfall profits from securing variances under existing zoning procedures.

Specific characteristics, apart from associated land use policies, will also serve to change the salience of land use planning under ZED to different interest groups. Landowners in areas designated for open space should welcome the compensation technique as insurance against loss in land value. On the other hand, the more numerous urban landholders who may be assessed for windfalls would undoubt-edly object and might overpower the landowners desiring compensa-tion. Realistically, ZED would not redistribute land value changes perfectly and uncertainty about the final distribution of benefits and costs might cause hesitancy on both sides. Restricted landowners might prefer the certainty of public purchase of their land, e.g., land banking, while those expecting to gain might pressure for more gen-eral sources of financing wipeout compensation, e.g., property taxes.

Builders and land developers may welcome new zoning techniques that offer to reduce the legal and political maneuvering associated with current zoning and zone-changing procedures. Moreover, once windfalls are collected or compensation paid, developers may feel more secure against arbitrary changes in use intensity that would harm their development efforts (Hagman 1976). Regardless of these positive aspects, builders and developers have invested substantially in learn-ing to work with and gaining access to the current system, and they may prefer the certainty of the known to the uncertainties of the new, especially if they have been successful in garnering windfalls from zone changes.

How will those who lend money for land development view the compensation and recapture of land value changes? Of necessity, they will have to be assured that the basic security of land value as mortgage collateral will remain intact. Therefore, they may require provisions to attach all wipeout compensation payments in loan agreements secured with land originally zoned for more intensive use. Basically, they should welcome the increased certainty of use for their land investments unless they, like some developers, envision losses from the decreasing probability of zone changes (Hagman 1976).

Local politicians might balk at supporting a ZED system for several reasons. The uncertainty of final outcomes may confuse their evalua-tion of political payoffs. They may be viewed as benefactors by those who receive compensation, but those assessed for windfalls will not be pleased. If the wipeouts to be compensated are clearly defined among a small group of politically active citizens while the windfalls are spread thinly over a larger, less active group, politicians may support ZED's introduction. The reverse conditions would probably not engender their support. Political support for ZED may also be lacking, at least privately, because the ability of politicans to grant windfalls and miti-gate wipeouts for politically influential constituents or interest groups will be reduced (Hagman 1976).

To conclude that the political acceptability of ZED is high or low solely on the basis of these potential effects is unwarranted. One point recurs frequently: uncertainty. Uncertainty usually causes parties affected to discount the desirability of a public policy. We have not specifically considered the level of government at which the political battle may be waged. If, as in Minnesota, a state enabling statute is considered, the influence of the traditional interest groups will vary from that in the local arena. The neighborhood groups may drop out, leaving a battle between the development and environmental coalitions. The result is impossible to predict. Perhaps ZED would be modified so that compensation would be provided, but only from general sources of financing.

SUMMARY AND IMPLICATIONS

Although introduced early in the twentieth century, the concept of zoning by eminent domain has not enjoyed widespread application. Until now, zoning under the police power has primarily served land use control objectives. But with the prospect of expanded land use control and consequent increases in windfalls and wipeouts, compensating the losers and assessing the winners should draw more attention in the political arena. In concept, ZED offers a mechanism to more completely weigh the benefits and costs of supplying certain public goods and strengthen the separation of "incompatible" uses while at least partially avoiding the redistribution of wealth that characterizes most zoning actions. However, as with any potential public policy, several questions about the actual performance of ZED raise doubts about its utility and political acceptability.

Perhaps the most serious area of concern is the ability of our property assessment system to accurately identify and measure land value changes caused by zoning actions. Without substantial new funding the task is probably impossible, and even with such funding it is not to be envied. Besides zoning actions, many market, private, and institutional forces also affect the value of land, but isolating the influence of zoning is crucial to the long-term viability of a ZED system. Imperfect assessment of any type would unleash the political wrath of those harmed and might hamper the land-market allocation system. Since windfalls would be more difficult to identify than wipeouts, the financial solvency of a ZED system would by no means be assured. Other specific characteristics of a ZED system such as timing, rate of value adjustment, corruption, and the level of administration required are problem areas that may also hinder ZED's success. There is no question that a ZED system could be instituted, but these issues point to problems that might hamper the attainment of land use planning objectives.

The potential benefits and costs of a ZED system are varied. There is reason to expect a decrease in "plan breaking" due to a decrease in opportunities to receive windfalls. ZED could also represent a significant improvement over direct regulation in providing certain public goods. Since the beneficiaries would be assessed and the providers compensated (at least partially), the tendency toward "oversupply" would be dampened. The most important cost may stem from the additional administrative and operational resources required for identifying, measuring, and adjusting land value changes.

The distributive effects of a ZED system are difficult to predict. If it operated as planned under full rates of recapture and compensation, the distribution of wealth in land after zoning action would be restored to that prevailing before. Assuming that lower-income groups receive fewer specific benefits and incur greater specific costs under traditional zoning, a move that maintained wealth levels could be considered an improvement.

Aspects of political acceptability of ZED are many and their importance impossible to predict, but the uncertainty attendant to introducing a novel land use technique may cause all affected parties to discount its desirability. The most vociferous political support for a ZED system may come from the coalition of environmental interest groups. However, their demand for publicly provided environmental goods may wane if the special assessments necessary to finance compensation fall on their property.

TDR is another technique recently proposed to simultaneously recapture the windfalls and compensate the wipeouts associated with public planning of land use. Chapter 7 is devoted to a treatment of the structure, issues, expected performance, and political acceptability of TDR.

✳ *Chapter 7*

Transferable Development Rights

Transferable Development Rights (TDRs) have recently been proposed as an additional device for implementing land use planning. Owners of land where development is restricted would be issued certificates in lieu of their foregone rights to develop. These certificates, known as TDRs, could then be sold (transferred) to those wishing to develop land at increased densities in other areas. The owner of the restricted land would thus be compensated by those who are permitted to develop. The attractiveness of this system lies in its potential for generating windfall-for-wipeout compensation through a market mechanism.

Compensation has become a central issue in land use planning for several reasons. For one thing, it may be required, or at least expedient, to avoid the legal obstacles presented by the taking issue.[1] As shown in Chapter 3, compensation may also be a means of providing more efficient allocation of land and related resources. For example, TDRs could be a direct mechanism whereby those who benefit from more esthetically pleasing urban growth pay those who bear the cost by being forced to keep their land in open space. Compensation devices such as TDRs may help to ensure equitable treatment of various groups affected by planning, and they may be essential in obtaining political acceptability for plans. These last three issues, equity, efficiency, and political acceptability, are the primary subjects of this evaluation.

1. See *The Taking Issue* by Bosselman, Callies, and Banta (1973). The authors indicate that there has been wide variability in court rulings on which types of public land use controls constitute unconstitutional taking of property.

In spite of the proliferation of materials and proposals related to TDRs, little explicit attention has been given to political acceptability.[2] The growing list of cases where legislation has been proposed but not approved casts doubt on this issue. Still, the TDR system appears to have strong political assets because it would compensate those who stand to be damaged by land use planning and thus reduce their opposition to planning and make it more acceptable to them. There is a certain basic appeal to equity in the system, too, since it would force the developers and urban landowners—the groups normally thought to receive large windfall profits from development—to pay those who are hurt.

Of course, paying from a windfall is paying from a surplus and represents no real (opportunity) cost to the developer or landowner. Does anyone then pay for TDRs? If we believe Schlaes (1974), nobody will have to pay. This is his conclusion based on an examination of the Chicago Plan for preserving historical landmarks with TDRs. But Schlaes envisions a situation where there is ample demand for increasing the density of new construction, without having to *down-zone*.[3] He also assumes a perfectly *elastic* demand for new buildings in the area to which the rights are to be transferred.[4] Our analysis will show that

2. A recent book edited by Rose, *The Transfer of Development Rights: A New Technique of Land Use Regulation* (1975) includes a variety of proposals and essays on TDRs. Articles by Costonis (1973) and by Chavooshian, Nieswand, and Norman (1974) were of particular importance in outlining the concept.

3. To *down-zone* is to change the zoning of property to a less intensive use than previously allowed. As used here, down-zoning usually means increasing the minimum lot size or reducing permitted density in some other way such as reducing the allowable floor area ratio.

4. *Elasticity* is an economic concept useful in understanding how TDRs and other land use planning devices can be expected to operate. The term here is used in a general sense. Demand curves and supply curves are termed "elastic" (Figure [a]) if they are relatively flat, meaning that small changes in price will produce large changes in the quantities demanded or supplied. When these curves are steeply sloped (Figure [b]), they are "inelastic"; even large changes in price will produce only modest changes in the quantities demanded or supplied.

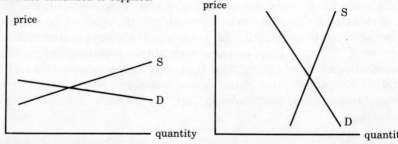

(a) Elastic demand and supply curves   (b) Inelastic demand and supply curves

Curves which are completely flat are "perfectly elastic," while those which go straight up and down are "perfectly inelastic."

these are crucial assumptions. These conditions may not exist in many cases, especially where TDRs are proposed as a means of preserving open space on urban peripheries.[5] This underscores the need to consider the specific market conditions in which TDRs are likely to be exchanged.

The few economic studies of TDRs to date have been concerned with the likely structure and mechanics of TDR markets. Barrows and Prenguber indicate that landowners may not be fully compensated for not being able to develop and that whether or not developers bear any of the costs depends upon the nature of the market for developed structures. They also underscore the importance of the relative bargaining strength of TDR holders and developers in areas where development is permitted (1975, p. 551). Field and Conrad also emphasize the importance of the relative bargaining strength of the affected parties and conclude that "in a poorly organized market, without an intermediary auctioneer, the lion's share of surplus would probably accrue to the developers" (1975, p. 339).

It is surprising that none of the economic analyses made to date have really paused to consider the economic nature of the goods TDRs would be used to produce.[6] Specifically, TDRs are being proposed as a means of employing land use planning for preserving open space, historical landmarks, and fragile ecological areas. With TDRs, it is claimed, land use planning could more effectively time growth and development (Rose 1975, pp. 8–10). Since these are public objectives, TDR is a means of producing *public goods*, i.e., something for the enjoyment of the public at large, or at least of some subgroup, and not for the use or consumption of any individual. Whether or not TDRs could efficiently provide such public goods is an issue neglected entirely in previous research, but one that shall be considered here.

As Chapter 5 indicates, traditional zoning may not be well suited for providing open space and similar public goods. Zoning makes no provision for dealing with the significant costs sustained by some landowners when their lands are excluded from development. Although this may be unfair treatment, it also provides these landowners with incentives to press for variances that permit their land to be developed. As more and more variances are granted, however, zoning plans are so completely changed that their original intent virtually disappears. Compensation devices such as TDRs and ZED (see Chapter 6) offer the hope of eliminating unfair treatment while reducing the incentive for

5. They probably don't exist even in Chicago and other metropolitan areas where excess supplies of office space in existing buildings are a recurring problem.

6. Studies include those by Schales (1974), Barrows and Prenguber (1975), and Field and Conrad (1975), already cited, plus those of Ishee (1974) and Clark (1974).

"plan breaking" that exists under zoning. Thus, TDRs might also be a means of strengthening zoning and making it work.

The next section provides a brief review and case histories of some TDR proposals. Alternative features in TDR system design will then be discussed, followed by an analysis of various conditions likely to occur in TDR markets. Several means of regulating markets are identified. The market analysis serves as a basis for discussing the efficiency of providing open space and other public goods with TDRs, as well as for commenting on issues relating to equity and political acceptability.

A REVIEW OF TDR PROGRAMS AND PROPOSALS

The first actual use of the TDR mechanism in the United States appears to have been the transfer of floor area ratio from one building to another in New York City as a means of preserving historic landmarks. Initially, New York City zoning regulations allowed the transfer of rights (permitted floor area ratio) between contiguous lots under the same ownership. Eventually, the regulations were modified to permit transfer to other lots in the immediate vicinity, and further modification enabled transfer to more distant areas of the city. These moves were made in an effort to ensure adequate demand for the rights to be transferred from the landmark buildings. In the view of Richards (1972), however, the modifications permitted transfer into areas already overly congested.

Washington, D.C. enacted a zoning ordinance in 1974 which provided for landmark preservation through the transfer of floor area ratios (Moore 1975, p. 231). A landmark preservation plan was proposed for Chicago by Costonis (1972), but this plan has never been adopted. Under the Chicago plan, transfers of floor area ratio would have been permitted from one building to another within the same landmark preservation district.

A proposal similar to the landmark preservation proposal has been made by Costonis and DeVoy (1974) for preserving fragile ecological areas in Puerto Rico. In this case, however, separate preservation areas ("protected environmental zones") and transfer areas, which could be quite distant from the preservation areas, would be created. Owners of land in the preservation areas would be compensated for loss of their development rights by being permitted to sell these rights to landowners in the development areas. "Transfers will not take place from office site to office site, each within a few blocks of the other . . . but from rainforest or baylands to downtown San Juan . . ." (Costonis and DeVoy 1974, p. 17).

TDRs have also been proposed as a means of accomplishing much broader purposes. Senate Bill No. 254, introduced in Maryland in 1972, would have used TDRs as the primary means of implementing statewide land use planning aimed at controlling urban sprawl and preserving open space. Under the proposed legislation, each county was required to draw up a master plan specifying "the percentage of remaining undeveloped land to be developed, and where development must take place" (Goodman 1972). Landowners would then issued a proportionate share of all development rights for the remaining development scheduled for the county based on the percentage of land area owned. No owner in any area designated for development would receive sufficient rights to develop all his land. Rather, he would have to purchase additional rights from owners of land in an area designated for preservation.

Similar legislation was also proposed for New Jersey but, again, never enacted. Municipalities would have been permitted to amend their zoning ordinances to create open space preservation districts. Whereas the Maryland proposal made use of the TDR approach compulsory throughout the state, drafters of the New Jersey bill viewed it only as enabling legislation. TDRs would have been issued to an owner of preserved land" . . . in an amount that represents the percentage of assessed value of his undeveloped land to the total value of all undeveloped land to be preserved in open space in the jurisdiction" (Rose 1975, p. 9). In contrast under the Maryland plan distribution was based on land area rather than value. The Maryland proposal envisioned separate TDR certificates for commercial property whereas the New Jersey plan did not (Rose 1975, p. 13).

Both the Maryland and New Jersey proposals used zoning or comprehensive plans to designate specific areas for preservation and development. In contrast, a proposal by Moore (1975) for TDRs in Virginia called for the *replacement* of zoning with a TDR system. Each community would set its desired population size *by referendum* and then estimate the number of dwelling units and commercial facilities required to serve such a population. These estimates would determine the total development rights requirements. Rights covering structures already in existence would be subtracted from them, and certificates for the balance would then be issued to the owners of all undeveloped land in the community in proportion to the amount of land held by each. Thus, the owner of a five-acre lot with residential potential would receive only a fraction of the rights required for full development of the parcel—in order to develop he would have to purchase the rest. No zoning plan would specify just where construction would take place, however. Rather, the developer would have to submit site development plans for approval, together with a sufficient number of TDRs, in order to be able to build on any specific site (Moore 1975, pp. 231–32). Thus, the primary objective of the Virginia plan was limiting population growth in specific areas rather than providing open space per se. Where the growth was to occur within these areas and which land was to remain undeveloped were decisions to be left more to the market—of course, subject to regulatory approval—than to some previous zoning plan.

Although several serious proposals have been made to use TDR as a means of preserving open space and controlling growth and development, TDR has been implemented in only one known case to date—the tiny hamlet (population 2304) of St. George, Vermont on the outskirts of rapidly expanding Burlington.[7] In May 1970 the municipality purchased 48 acres of land in a designated development area. To purchase this land from the community and obtain the right to develop it, a developer must also purchase development rights to land outside the central area whose owners are thus compensated for having their land continue in nonintensive use (Wilson 1974).

ALTERNATIVES IN TDR SYSTEM DESIGN

The preceding discussion illustrates that TDR is not a narrowly defined concept. Its purposes can be as diverse as landmark preservation and controlling urban growth. There are also a number of significant variations in how a TDR system might be structured.

Several of the structural issues have already been noted. For example, it is possible to use TDR strictly in conjunction with zoning. Where a zoning plan specifies the permitted uses for every plot of land, TDR becomes merely a means of compensating those zoned out of development by those who are zoned in. As in the Virginia plan, however, TDRs might be used as a means of partially eliminating zoning. The overall development potential of an area would be specified, but where development is to occur (or be clustered) within the area would depend more upon private, market-oriented decision-makers. Their decisions would determine who buys TDRs and who sells them and thus who compensates or is compensated. This latter TDR design would have many of the attributes of the cluster and planned unit developments that have been permitted in some communities since the early 1960s.

Rights to Be Covered

In some proposed systems, TDRs would be issued only to cover the development potential or rights eliminated in the preservation zone

7. As of July 1976.

(Costonis 1973). In others (Ishee 1974, Chavoosian, Nieswand, and Norman 1974), however, rights would be issued to cover not only all pre-TDR development potential in the preservation zone but also the residual (permitted but unused) densities in the development zone. Developers would then be at liberty to transfer rights within the development zone as well as from the preservation zone. This second system could lead to much denser development in some parts of the development zone and would produce results similar to TDRs without zoning, as described above, except that here clusters of development would occur only in a development zone and not throughout the area covered by the plan.

The Number of Development Rights

How many rights are to be issued initially? This may be the crucial factor in determining the ultimate performance of the TDR market. If too many are issued relative to the amount of development to occur in a given TDR jurisdiction and if price determination is left to an unregulated market, price per unit for TDRs may be low, giving rise to complaints of unfairness and "taking" on the part of rights holders.[8]

A common proposal is to issue enough TDRs to cover the entire (as yet unexercised) development potential of the development zone (Chavooshian, Norman, and Nieswand 1974, Ishee 1974). Existing zoning ordinances usually leave substantial latitude to developers, and there is so much "slack" built into these plans that the bulk of development that could potentially be carried out is much greater than will actually take place. Thus, if TDRs are issued to cover so much development potential, many of them will never be used (Barrows and Prenguber 1975, p. 550).

Specification of the Conversion Factor

In one respect, the number of TDRs issued may not be of such great importance. It will be necessary for the legislation and ordinances under which a TDR system operates to specify the rate at which TDRs may be converted into additional building structures (the *conversion factor*). Lowering the conversion factor would lower the effective amount of development possible with a given number of TDRs. It might also be possible to change the conversion factor after a TDR system has been initiated thus maintaining control over the market for TDRs to help encourage desired performance should the market function poorly (Field and Conrad 1975).

8. Strictly speaking of course, compensation will be equal to the quantity of rights a landowner receives times the price per unit. As will be shown below, price is determined by the quantity of rights issued and other factors, including the rate at which these rights may be converted.

In practice, it could be possible to have several different series of TDRs, one for each different type of development permitted in the development zone—an approach envisioned in some proposals for TDR systems (Moore 1975, Ishee 1974, Goodman 1972). With this approach, there could be one series of TDRs for residential construction, one for commercial buildings, and another for industrial structures. This would mean three separate markets and three separate regulation problems, however, and the alternative of having one basic series of TDRs and separate conversion factors seems more tractable. In a system with separate conversion factors, for example, residential and commercial buildings might have factors of one and five respectively, indicating that each additional residential unit would require one TDR whereas each additional 1,000 feet of commercial space would require five. With such a system there would probably be less chance of market concentration and monopolistic pricing in the commercial and industrial land markets where fewer sales are transacted.

Basis for Distribution

Another set of alternatives that must be faced in setting up a TDR system concerns the basis on which the transferable rights are to be distributed. The idea underlying TDRs is that they are to provide an automatic means of compensating landowners for the development potential (rights) eliminated by zoning ordinances and associated density restrictions. In some cases, where uncontested zoning plans have been in effect in a preservation zone and where the effect of preservation is merely to reduce permitted maximum densities, the calculation of lost potential is straightforward. For example, if the permitted floor area ratio is to be reduced from 18 to 10 in order to preserve a historic landmark on a certain lot, then the loss of potential is clearly eight.

In the case of open areas which are to be preserved, however, determining development potential is a difficult, if not impossible task. Three approaches have been suggested. One is to estimate the development potential of lands in the preservation zone on the basis of a survey of their physical attributes (Wengert and Graham 1974). A second approach is to distribute TDRs in proportion to the land areas involved (Ishee 1974, Moore 1975), and the third in proportion to current market land values (Chavooshian, Nieswand, and Norman 1974, Rose 1974). Each of these approaches has its difficulties.

While physical attributes have great bearing on development potential, they are not its sole determinants. Furthermore, making detailed physical surveys is both time consuming and costly. Land areas, on the other hand, are easily measured, but a well-sited 20-acre plot may be prime land for a shopping center whereas the swampy 640-acre tract two miles down the road may never be suited for anything but the pasture for which it is currently used. A plan based on a strict land area distribution, however, would give the 640-acre plot 32 times as many development rights.

Market land values appear to offer a more acceptable basis for distribution in many respects. Trained land appraisers and tax assessors capable of assessing current market values can be found in many areas of the country. Appraisals are quick and relatively inexpensive, especially when carried out in large numbers for the same area. Furthermore, tax rolls in many states already carry reasonably accurate market value assessments.

There is one potential pitfall with distribution based on market values, however, that most studies of TDRs appear to have ignored. *If TDRs are to be distributed according to market values, the basis must be reduction in market values, not total market values,* for it is the reduction in market values that best reflects the loss in development potential. For example, take the case of three one-acre plots of land, the first valued at $600, the second at $900, and the third at $1,500. Assume that 30 development rights are to be distributed among their owners to compensate them for having their lands zoned for agricultural use only. Assume also that the agricultural value of each acre is $500 and that, miraculously, the price of TDRs on the market turns out to be $50 each, thus generating exactly enough value to compensate the three landowners for their aggregate wipeout of $1,500.

If the TDRs are distributed in proportion to total market values, the first landowner receives six worth $300, the second nine worth $450, and the third fifteen worth $750. Counting both the agricultural value of land and the value of TDRs received, the first landowner is left with $800, the second with $950, and third with $1250. The first two gain and the third—the one initially holding the most valuable land—loses.[9] If the TDRs were based on the projected decrease in land values, however, the landowners would receive two, eight, and 20 units, leaving their total asset values unchanged by the introduction of TDRs.

The question of ultimate TDR price determination is also crucial. If the price in the preceding example had been less than $50 (assuming that TDRs are distributed in proportion to market value reduction) all three landowners would have been made worse off by the introduction of the TDR system. If the price had been greater than $50, all would have been made better off. In the following section, we discuss price determination.

9. If distribution based on land area had been used, each land owner would have received 10 TDRs worth $500, giving him a total value of $1000. The redistribution would have been even more skewed in favor of owners of cheaper land.

THE MARKET FOR TRANSFERABLE
DEVELOPMENT RIGHTS

How well TDR systems function will ultimately be determined by how the TDR market works. This will depend upon the behavior of several associated markets. Once TDRs have been distributed, they will be demanded by developers as substitutes for land. That is , by purchasing TDRs builders will be permitted to exceed the maximum densities otherwise allowed. Thus, they will require less land per unit of housing, and TDRs become, in effect, land substitutes. How strongly TDRs are demanded thus depends upon the price of land relative to that of TDRs and upon the extent to which the maximum densities permitted without TDRs actually force developers to use more land than they would otherwise choose to do. TDR demand also depends upon the demand for the housing or commercial and industrial buildings developers produce. The observations made in the following sections assume a perfect market for a single product called housing. The assumption of a perfect market is then relaxed in order to examine the impact of various types of market concentration and bargaining situations on the TDR market.

The Housing Developer and the Demand
for TDRs

Consider a developer who produces houses of uniform quality. If his operation is small relative to the total market, he will view the selling price of these houses as fixed. He will choose different combinations of land and building structure to produce a house, and his final choice will depend upon the relative prices of land and structure. If land is relatively cheap, he will use more land and less structure and vice versa.

If the developer is not subject to any legal restrictions on the size of the lot he may use for building a house, he will tend to build houses on smaller lots as the price of land rises, thus increasing density. When local zoning plans, annexations, and decisions on the provision of public services limit the amount (supply) of land available for urban development, the supply price rises, and density increases.

Zoning ordinances typically do more than designate which lands may be used for housing and which for other activities. They also specify that certain areas are to be used for single and others for multiple dwelling units. They further require a minimum lot size for a building of a certain number of dwelling units. Minimum lot sizes constitute maximum density regulations.[10] Thus, although the price of

---

10. Zoning which specifies minimum lot sizes for residences and maximum floor area to land ratios for commercial and industrial structures is known as *denisty zoning* (Costonis 1973).

land may dictate that the developer build densely, he may not exceed the maximum density limit. He is thus forced to use more land (and provide less structure) than the relative prices would otherwise indicate, and the cost of the housing which he produces will increase.[11] Of course, the feasibility of producing at a higher cost depends ultimately on the market price of housing.

TDRs would provide the developer with a means of increasing density beyond the maximum or residual densities otherwise permitted by the zoning ordinance. This means that *the developer's demand for TDRs is ultimately derived from his incentive to have the permitted density increased. If the relative price of land is too low or if for other reasons the maximum density restrictions are ineffective, there will be no significant demand for TDRs.*[12]

The importance of land price and maximum density restriction can be illustrated diagrammatically.[13] Figure 7.1 depicts a unit isoquant for housing construction, II_0, which represents all of the possible combinations of land (l) and (s) required to build one house of the same quality. "Structure" is a composite of all items other than land required to build a house. AB is the "price line," its slope representing the relative prices of land and structure. With no maximum density (minimum lot size) regulations on construction, a developer decides to build his uniform quality houses with l_0 units of land and s_0 units of structure. If the zoning ordinance or building code is amended to require a minimum of l_1 units of land per house (a maximum density limit of $1/l_1$ houses per acre), the developer now works with the modified isoquant II_1. In this case, however, the minimum lot size, l_1, is not effective in changing the developer's decision. But if the minimum lot size is changed to l_2, causing the isoquant to change to II_2, the developer would decide to build houses with l_2 units of land and s_2 units of structure. Thus, the minimum lot size l_2 is an effective limit. Costs are increased by $(AA') \times p_l$, where p_l is the price of land. It is the incentive to reduce this cost increase which causes the developer to demand TDRs. If the initial price of land had been higher, however, causing the price line to be CD rather than AB, TDRs would have been demanded even at the lower density restriction, l_1. Thus, the price of land also

11. The option of building lower-quality units is excluded by the assumption of the present analysis.

12. For example, if housing development areas in neighboring counties or municipalities are less restrictively zoned, development activities may shift precipitously to those areas as density limits in the jurisdiction are approached. This is tantamount to saying that demand for housing can be highly elastic within a given planning jurisdiction.

13. This paragraph presents a technical description of the effects of density regulations on the homebuilder's decision-making. Together with Figure 7.1, it may safely be omitted by the reader who is less interested in economic details.

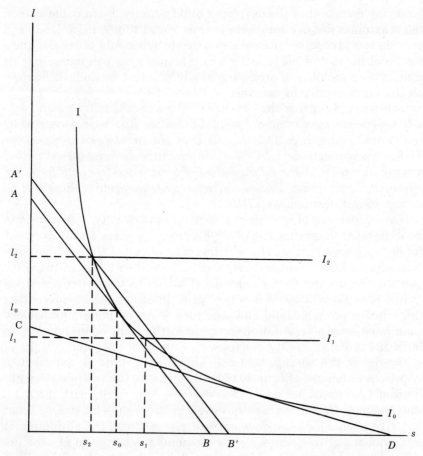

Figure 7.1.   Unit isoquant illustrating the effect of maximum density restriction on the use of land (*l*) and structure (*s*) in housing construction.

helps to determine whether or not the developer will wish to purchase TDRs.

In summary, the developer's demand for transferable development rights (r_d) may be stated in functional notation,

$$r_d = f(p_r, p_h, p_l, p_s, k_0, k_1) \qquad (7.1)$$

where

p_r = the price of rights
p_h = the price of housing

p_l = the price of land
p_s = the price of building structure
k_0 = the residual or maximum density limit and
k_1 = the rights conversion factor.

The quantity of rights demanded can be expected to decrease with increases in p_r and increase with increases in p_h and p_l.

The developer operates according to a constraint on the number of houses (h) he may build,

$$h \leq k_0 l + k_1 r \qquad (7.2)$$

where l and r represent the quantity of land and TDRs he will devote to a given development. Residual densities, k_0, must be lower than some threshold level in order for any rights to be demanded. To be specific, the demand for rights will be zero unless

$$p_r/k_1 < p_l/k_0 \qquad (7.3)$$

which merely states that the price of rights must be less than the price of the land required to produce a given amount of housing, considering the rate at which TDRs may legally be exchanged for permission to build at greater density.

The developer, as indicated above, will also demand land (l) and "structures" (s) in his production process, with the strength of his demand for each of these factors depending on the same factors as in equation (7.1) above. Market demands for rights, land, and structures will be the sum of the demands for the individual developers and again will depend upon the same factors included in equation (7.1).

The Supply of TDRs

At the market level, prices will not be fixed. They will vary according to the aggregate quantity of the factors used. The nature of the supply of development rights is difficult to specify in view of the lack of previous experience. We can note, however, that once rights are issued, they become assets separate from land. They have many of the characteristics of an exhaustible natural resource. As such, we know that their current supply price is partially a function of expectations for future market conditions. Some holders of TDRs can be expected to retain them for future sales if they expect the price to rise in the future.

In the absence of previous market experience with TDRs, holders may tend to set an initial reservation price corresponding to the amount they feel their land values have been reduced by restrictions in the preservation area. Field and Conrad (1975) suggested that the market supply of TDRs would slope upward from TDR holders' initial reservation price level, $\bar{p}_r$, and become perfectly inelastic at the point where the total number r_T of TDRs is exhausted. Such a fixed stock supply schedule is pictured in Figure 7.2. It is consistent with the notion of a fixed natural resource supply schedule.

The price, $\bar{p}_r$, which people initially expect for their TDRs will be based largely upon prices paid for land converted to urban uses during preceding years. This process will have been gradual, limited by the rate of expansion of urban boundaries. Now, however, TDRs from all open space will be available at once, potentially for immediate use. It seems likely that the reservation price, $\bar{p}_r$, may well exceed the initial market clearing price. Recent research on preferential property taxa-

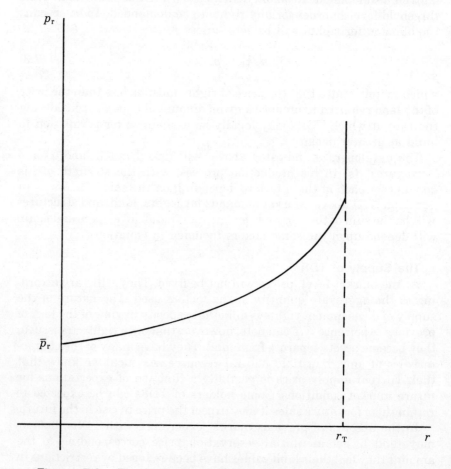

Figure 7.2. The supply of transferable development rights.

tion on urban fringe lands in California tends to substantiate the idea that the owners of undeveloped fringe lands have a tendency to over-value their lands relative to realistic market expectations (Hansen and Schwartz 1975). This lends credence to claim that those issued TDRs may initially have unrealistic ideas of their value.

There are other reasons to believe that considerable instability may arise in the supply of TDRs during the period just after they have been issued. Landowners issued TDRs will receive an asset with charac-teristics substantially different from those of the land they have been holding. The risk picture will be different from that associated with land, and uncertainties about the future of the TDR market will be extremely high, causing some to liquidate their holdings. When TDRs are assigned to mortgaged land, some sales may be delayed until legal difficulties are cleared up and arrangements made with creditors. All these factors may combine to make TDR supply highly unstable at first. Eventually, however, landowners with desire to hold their newly created assets will sell them, experience with the market will accumu-late, and the legal status of the new instruments will be clarified. Then the behavior of suppliers can be expected to stabilize, and supply will take on the characteristics shown in Figure 7.2.

An Overview of the Market and
Its Regulation

Whether or not the TDR system will accomplish its stated objectives depends heavily on how the market functions. The discussion of supply and demand can now be used to penetrate this issue more deeply. The interaction of supply and demand determines both the price of TDRs and the quantity traded and thus the total compensation generated. A number of factors were identified above as important to this market. Some of them may be subject to variation in regulation of the market.

The market for urban land is important for two reasons. First, the price of urban land must be high enough to encourage developers to build at relatively high densities. Zoning and other restrictions on the supply of land will tend to boost prices, but high prices will not be sufficient to guarantee a demand for TDRs. There must also be effec-tive legal restrictions on the density of development permitted in the development zone without TDRs. Thus, in addition to limiting the supply of land in the development zone, it may also be necessary to down-zone the remaining land by increasing minimum lot sizes or to use some other variant of density zoning.[14]

14. Costonis (1973) outlined the legal difficulties associated with down-zoning and concluded that they are not insurmountable. See note 3 for a definition of down-zoning.

The demand for TDRs will also be affected by their price and by the conversion factors or rates at which they may be exchanged for increased development densities. Price will be determined jointly by demand and supply. Supply will depend upon the number of TDRs issued, recipients' initial liquidity needs, and their expectations for future market behavior. The number of TDRs issued and the conversion factors are important determinants that must be set when a market is initiated. Given the lack of past experience with TDR market behavior, it will be difficult to decide upon the appropriate magnitudes. If too many rights are issued and/or the conversion factor is too low, price may well be too low to provide "reasonable compensation" to landowners in the preservation zone. If too few rights are issued and /or the conversion factor is too high, overcompensation may occur to the detriment of both developers, who may be forced out of business, and homebuyers, who will have to pay higher prices.

The nature of the demand for housing or other developed structures will be crucial in TDR market behavior. Initially, if there is little demand for development in a given market area, demand for TDRs will also be small. Obviously, such a market would not support a large preservation area. If housing demand is highly elastic, such measures as the reduction of residual densities—designed to insure an adequate market for TDRs—may increase housing costs enough to cut back drastically on the demand for housing and thus reduce the derived demand for TDRs. If the supply price of TDRs is flexible, it may drop, making TDRs cheaper as a substitute for land and thus reducing the cost of housing. In this case, demand for housing and for TDRs would be partially restored.

Demand for housing and other buildings should be quite elastic in market areas where buyers have nearby alternatives, as is the case in one municipality or one county in a large metropolitan area. Such a jurisdiction would not have good prospects for establishing TDRs without the participation of other governments in the same area, especially where it would be necessary to reduce exisiting density limitations and thus increase overall development costs in an attempt to create a TDR market. If, however, existing density limits were already providing effective barriers to additional development at the time a TDR system was established, the cost-reducing factors of the TDRs might even stimulate the local development market.

Where a demand for new housing tends to be price inelastic, there will be a greater possibility of creating an adequate market for TDRs, although total housing costs may be increased in the process. Housing demand should be more elastic in large metropolitan areas generally and inelastic in relatively isolated smaller communities.

Regulation of an Ongoing TDR Market

Once a TDR market is established, it will be necessary to regulate its behavior. This necessity is likely to arise either because it was not possible in advance to determine the necessary market parameters with sufficient accuracy to insure desirable market behavior or because conditions affecting the development market change with the passage of time and thus cause changes in the TDR system.

Four "levers" may be singled out as potential means of changing market behavior:

1. raise or lower the residual density factor (k_0), which stipulates the maximum density permitted without purchasing TDRs, thus shifting their demand,
2. change the conversion factor (k_1), which specifies the rate at which TDRs may be converted into permits for increased density, again shifting demand,
3. increase or decrease the number of TDRs in circulation, thus shifting their supply schedule, or
4. change the amount of land available for development, thus shifting the land supply schedule.

The political and legal feasibility of making such changes may be subject to doubt in many instances, depending on which of the four "levers" is moved and in which direction it is moved. However, failure to change the market in many cases will produce political pressures that could also be untenable. The political feasibility of these measures, would depend on the relative strength of TDR holders as a group versus that of the other groups, including urban landowners, developers, and homebuyers who might stand to gain.

If TDR prices are low, those who hold them—i.e., landowners in the preservation area—may claim that their rights have been taken without just compensation. It may then be necessary for the regulating body to buy up some of the outstanding TDRs at what could be an extensive cost to the public.[15] Where land is to be rezoned from development to preservation status to increase TDR demand, and where this required compensating the owners with TDRs in keeping with the spirit of the system, the net effect could be an even greater lowering of price. Attempting to increase price by down-zoning land in the development area, i.e., decreasing k_0, may raise legal questions (Costonis 1973) if this issue was not addressed at the time the market was initially

---

15. Some proposed TDR systems have the land control authority or some other public body serve this function on a continuous basis.

established. The final regulatory possibility, decreasing the TDR conversion factors and thus requiring more TDRs per additional unit developed, seems feasible. The effectiveness of this measure, however, would depend heavily on the elasticity of the supply of land as well as on the elasticity of the demand for housing.[16] Impacts of these regulatory approaches will vary accordingly. The additional costs of TDRs would tend to be borne by homebuyers if housing demand is inelastic, by urban landowners if the supply of urban land is inelastic, and by developers forced out of business if both the supply of land and demand for housing are elastic.

Serious questions arise about the ability of the regulative authority to remove some TDRs from the market through purchase should this be necessary to improve the market. If a public body is to purchase rights, where will the money to do so come from? If the initial TDR system is poorly constructed and the reduction in value of lands in the preservation area is too large relative to the potential of the development zone, large public purchases might have to be made before TDR holders feel that they are adequately compensated. Would funds for such purchases come from general tax levies? If the development market turns out to be too small to bear the burden of TDR purchases, special assessments of newly developed properties would not be likely to generate sufficient revenues either.

When the TDR price rises, publicly held rights could then be sold. It is even possible that a public body might be vested with the authority to print and sell additional rights should this prove to be desirable market regulation. If a public body to buy and sell TDRs could be funded, its activity might meet the need for regulatory changes in the TDR market. In particular, it might serve to bring the market through its initial period of supply instability and by its activities dispel some of the uncertainties that might scare TDR holders into dumping their assets on the market.

The legality of giving the TDR marketing body the authority to issue new rights would undoubtedly be challenged and would ultimately depend upon court interpretations of whether or not the initial issuing of TDRs to landowners in the preservation area constituted a final severance of their right to develop their property. If this interpretation were to hold up in the courts, this could be tantamount to recognition that the right to develop has beeen transferred to the public sphere (with once-and-for-all compensation). This rationale

16. See Muth (1968) for a full exposition of the interrelationship of the elasticity of supply of land and the demand elasticity for housing in determining land and housing prices.

could serve as possible justification for the public to sell new development rights. Public officials might view this as an attractive new source of revenue.[17]

Imperfections in TDR Markets

Other writers have pointed to the possibility for imperfections to arise in TDR markets (Barrows and Prenguber 1975, Field and Conrad 1975). If the number of participants involved in any of the groups interacting in the market is small, the actions of individuals could potentially influence and, to some degree, control the market.

When the preservation area is relatively small, as may occur in the case of historic landmarks or critical environmental areas, the number of people issued TDRs could be small, giving them oligopolistic powers that would increase the price and reduce the volume of TDRs traded and result in either higher development costs or lower land prices than would otherwise occur. In most cases of landmark preservation, however, the number of rights would be so small relative to the market for new development that little overall impact would result.

On the buyer's side, if the number of developers is small, they would tend to behave oligopsonistically, demanding fewer TDRs and paying lower prices than they would in a perfect market situation. There indeed often may be relatively few developers, especially for commercial and industrial construction. Field and Conrad concluded that without some government agency to act as an intermediary auctioneer, developers would probably capture the major part of the "surplus" in the TDR market (1975, p. 339).

If the number of both sellers and buyers is low, the possibility of bilateral oligopoly exists wherein bargaining strategies would assume great importance and the final outcome of the market would be quite indeterminate. This is the case described by Barrows and Prenguber (1975, p. 556).

While the danger of noncompetitive behavior in TDR markets is high it is also possible in some instances that TDRs would add to the competitiveness of already concentrated urban land markets. They might provide buyers with an alternative to purchasing additional land, and, when land prices are high, as would occur when landowners control the market, this would provide an extra incentive for the purchase of TDRs as a land substitute.

17. In fact, in some respects, it is similar to revenue generating schemes suggested for New York City whereby the city government would be permitted to sell floor area ratio for some of its buildings to permit development in other areas of the city (Richards 1972).

HOW WELL WILL THE TDR
SYSTEM PERFORM?

This chapter has emphasized identifying the groups likely to be affected by planning under a TDR system. These are, for the most part, the same as the groups identified in Chapter 5 for an interest in Zoning by Eminent Domain. They include owners of land restricted in use, owners of land in development areas, developers, and renters and buyers of houses and other new structures. Environmental and neighborhood groups also have an interest in the system since it will promote either open space or increased development and congestion.

The distribution of the impacts under TDR will determine the equity of the system. By clarifying the nature of this distribution we can also help to generate an understanding of the likely political acceptability of TDRs. Finally, the distribution of benefits and costs is important even in determining whether or not TDRs can lead to the efficient provision of such public goods as open space and the preservation of critical natural areas. These topics will now be discussed with specific reference to distribution.

Windfalls and Wipeouts

Hagman (1975), Rose (1975), and most others who have written on TDRs emphasize the importance of the windfall-for-wipeout feature of the system. We believe that this aspect should be deemphasized for a number of reasons. To begin with, it is difficult to establish what constitutes a windfall or a wipeout, and even if the concept could be clarified, measurement would be difficult. Second, the windfall-for-wipeout expression implies that windfalls could be expected to equal wipeouts, and this is definitely not the case. Finally, referring to payments made for TDRs as "windfall recapture" leads one to believe that such payment would be made only from windfalls, and that is not necessarily true either.

Windfalls and wipeouts are difficult to define since individual views on what is earned and what is not earned differ. If Jones buys a piece of land today and a new highway is built nearby next year causing the land value to double, Smith thinks Jones got a windfall. Jones, who shopped for the land for several years and devoted substantial time and expense to learning about likely growth patterns, may feel that he earned his money and that he has provided a valuable service to society by acquiring the land and setting it aside for future use. Smith, a farmer who owns land in a nearby area recently zoned for agricultural use only, feels that he has been "wiped out" by the zoning ordinance. Several farms in his area were sold to speculators at high prices in recent years, and his farm had been assessed at a higher value than could be justified for farmland. The truth of the matter is, however, that nobody ever made Smith an offer since his farm does not have a scenic view. Was he really "wiped out," and if so, how does one measure his wipeout?

Assuming for a moment that we can agree on what is meant by windfalls and wipeouts, their values need not be—probably never would be—equal and offsetting. Figure 7.3 depicts the land markets for an area zoned for preservation and an adjacent area zoned for de-

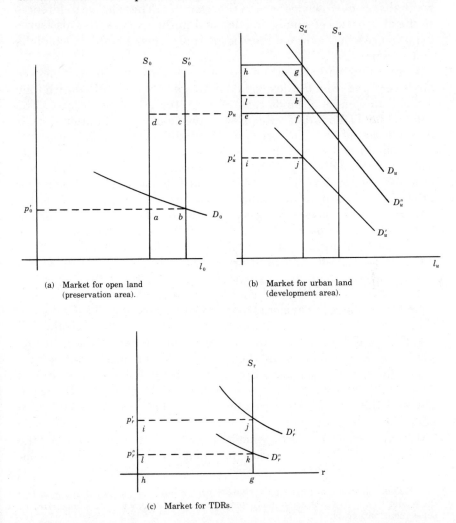

(a) Market for open land (preservation area).

(b) Market for urban land (development area).

(c) Market for TDRs.

Figure 7.3. An illustration of TDRs, windfalls, and wipeouts.

velopment.[18] For clarity, supplies of land in the two are assumed to be perfectly inelastic but the analysis does not depend on this. The zoning action causes some developable lands to be shifted to the undevelopable category, causing a net loss (wipeout) equal to the area *abcd* to preservation landowners. On the other hand, owners of developable land enjoy a gain (windfall), area *efgh*, caused by the restriction. No relationship between the markets requires the two magnitudes to be equal. A similar diagram would show that the greater the area set aside for open space, the more likely that wipeouts would exceed windfalls, as narrowly defined in this example. The relative differences in the elasticities of supply and demand in the two markets also serve to influence whether or not there is great divergence between windfalls and wipeouts.

Continuing with the same example, assume now that owners of lands removed from the development area are issued TDRs which they can sell to owners of lands remaining in the development area. The demand for TDRs is determined, as defined earlier in equation (7.1). It is a function of the *TDR* price, p_r, the residual density k_0, the rights conversion factor k_1, and the prices of urban land p_u and housing p_h. It does not depend directly or strictly on the size of any windfall received by urban landowners. The availability of TDRs causes the demand for urban land D_u to shift downward, since they are substituted for land. This reduces the payments received by these landowners in proportion to the magnitude of the shift. If the maximum density limits in the urban area are quite restrictive, the demand for urban land will shift strongly downward, and high prices will be paid for TDRs, with a correspondingly high drop in land payment. Such a shift is shown in Figure 7.3(b), with the demand for land shifting to D_u'. In this example, the loss in payments to landowners caused by TDR substitution is equal to area, *hgji*, which greatly exceeds the hypothetical windfall gain, *efgh*, which initially resulted from restricting land supply in the development zone. Had the maximum density limit permitted in the development zone been less binding, however, the shift in demand for land would have been less marked, say to D''_u, for example, and the loss, *hglk,* in payments to landowners could well have been less than their gain.

In summary of the above, windfalls need not equal wipeouts, and the introduction of TDRs may reduce payments to landowners (or develop-

18. This and the following paragraphs discussing Figure 7.3 may be safely omitted by the reader who is less interested in economic detail. The arguments are summarized in subsequent paragraphs.

ers) receiving windfalls by less or more than the value of their windfall. From this it follows that there is no basis whatsoever to expect that payments to TDR holders will offset the wipeouts from restrictions on the use of their land.

It can be shown, under quite restrictive assumptions, that payments received by TDR holders will exactly equal the reduction in payments to owners of land scheduled for development. If, as has already been assumed, the supply, S_u, of land is perfectly inelastic, and if the TDR supply, S_r, is also inelastic, then the payments will be equal provided that (1) factors of production other than land may be bought at constant prices, (2) the market demand for housing is totally inelastic, and (3) there are numerous buyers and sellers in the markets for land and housing. Based on these highly unrealistic assumptions, Figure 7.3(c) illustrates the case where payments received by TDR holders equal the reduced payments to urban landowners. Note, however, that neither of the total payments, *hglk*, or, *hgij*, is equal to the losses, *abcd*, which TDR holders suffer as preservation area landowners.

Figure 7.3 may be used to illustrate one more important point: *It is entirely possible for TDRs to result in wipeout-for-wipeout compensation rather than windfall-for-wipeout.* In the case where residual density limits are quite restrictive, causing the demand for urban land to drop strongly after TDRs become available, the price for such land could actually drop to a level, p_u', below that established before rezoning, p_u, thus causing urban landholders to claim that they have been wiped out in order to compensate owners of restricted lands for their losses. In Figure 7.3(b), if demand drops to D_u' as TDRs are purchased, area *efij* could be considered the total wipeout for landowners unfortunate enough not to be restricted to the preservation area.

TDRs and Variance Proceedings

Will TDRs remove the incentive for landholders in preservation areas to seek the zoning changes which, in the long run, tend to render zoning ineffective? This should depend somewhat on the price differential that remains between urban land and rural land on the periphery after TDRs have been established. The example and discussion in the preceding section show that there is no automatic mechanism under TDRs to equalize land prices in the two markets. If an owner of land in the preservation area can still obtain a higher price for it by obtaining a variance to include it in the development zone, he could benefit from so doing. The fact that he has been compensated once through the sale of TDRs would constitute at best a moral deterrent. On the other hand, officials in charge of variance proceedings may have much stronger reasons for denying such a petition. Certainly the landowner would now be on weaker ground in claiming illegal taking of his property rights.

TDRs, Public Goods, and Efficiency

The twofold purpose of TDRs is to strengthen zoning as a device for preserving open space and critical natural areas and to permit zoning to do a better job of controlling land conversion for development. Open space and critical natural areas are, in effect, public goods, as explained earlier. They are not likely to be provided by the private market in sufficient quantities since many of their benefits do not accrue to the owners of the land but are enjoyed by the public at large. Thus, the ultimate justification for zoning as a means of providing more open space and preserving landmarks and critical ecological areas is that the market fails to provide enough of them. The question is, does the TDR mechanism permit zoning to accomplish this task more efficiently?

Figure 7.4 depicts a market for open lands where the total (social) demand is D_0^T. D_0^T represents the aggregation of the private market demand for the land in nonintensive production uses such as agriculture, D_0^M, and the (external) public benefits from holding the land in open space, D_0^P. The unrestricted market for land would retain l_0^0 in open spaces, whereas the socially efficient optimum would require l_0'. Zoning represents an attempt to restructure and increase the supply of land to provide additional open space.

If planning and zoning officials had perfect knowledge of people's preferences (and a perfect understanding of land supply) they could shift supply to S_0', causing exactly the right amount of additional land to be set aside. Without compensation, owners of land currently outside the range of development and owners of currently developable land who have their rights restricted would pay the cost of providing the additional open space—the former by having their land prices depressed and the latter by being forced to sell or rent for nonintensive use.

When landowners bear the full brunt of the cost of providing open space, the general public who enjoy the open space—with the exception of those who may pay higher rents and higher prices for new buildings—get the good they want for nothing. To be more precise, they get it for the cost of participating and exerting their influence in the planning and zoning process. Because they pay no other costs, they can be expected to "overreport" their demands for open space. Owners of land remaining in development zones[19] will receive an extra benefit

---

19. Including those who have already developed properties there.

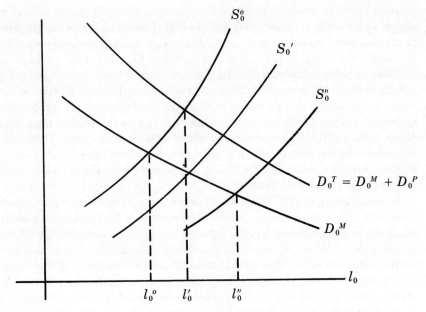

(a) Market and total social demands for open lands.

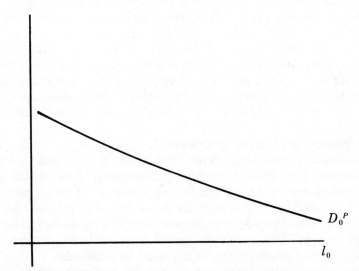

(b) Demand for open space (land) as a public good.

Figure 7.4. Land use planning and the demand for public goods.

as land there increases in value. They reap a windfall, presumably, in addition to enjoying free open space. If the demand for purchase and rental of new housing and other buildings is not perfectly elastic, consumers of these items will pay somewhat higher prices, perhaps to the extent of paying more than the additional open space is really worth to them. It is possible that open space would be overprovided in such a situation if environmentalists and neighborhood protection groups, fortified by those owning land in the development area, are more influential than landowners in the preservation zone. If restrictions on development result in shifting the supply of open lands to S_0'', in the example shown in Figure 7.4, l_0'' would be provided rather than the optimal amount of land, l_0'.

It is not clear that TDRs would add to the efficiency of public goods provision through zoning. In a carefully designed TDR system losses to the owners of restricted lands might be reduced or eliminated without causing any net loss to owners of developable land. This would theoretically neutralize the influence of landowners on either side of the issue. The public at large, who presumably want more open space, would be split between those who already own housing and other buildings and those who rent or plan to buy new buildings. The latter group might still have to pay for open space in the form of higher prices and rents, which would stand to benefit owners. Special environmental and neighborhood groups could still benefit from more open space without having to pay anything except the costs of participation. In other words, the introduction of TDR does not in itself constitute a cost–benefit equilibrating device, and efficiency is still left to the political arena. However, to the extent that the generalizations provided in Chapter 4 are correct, the political arena is not concerned with efficiency.

The Reduction of External Effects

The preceding argument shows that public goods, such as open space, are really one form of externality. The farmer, for example, who farms land on the urban periphery provides open space of value to urban residents, but for this external benefit (and in this case also a public good) he is typically not compensated. The discussion of public goods shows that TDRs are not designed to reward the farmer in direct proportion to the external benefit his open land provides.

TDRs are not designed to eliminate or reduce technical externalities per se. Rather, as we have indicated, they are viewed primarily as a strengthening device for zoning. To the extent that they enable zoning to control development and concentrate it in certain areas, then they can be expected to contribute to reducing the negative effects of de-

velopment. But in general, TDRs can be no more effective in eliminating these externalities than the zoning ordinances they are used to
enforce.

Congestion in urban areas is another externality that zoning typically tries to address. *The TDR system might actually increase urban
congestion.* In order to create a market for TDRs, as we have seen,
additional development must be permitted in certain urban areas. In
buying TDRs, developers and landowners in these areas are in effect
buying permission to exceed the existing maximum densities. If these
areas are already heavily developed, the social costs of additional
congestion may be high. This is Richards' (1972) criticism of the TDR
system in New York.

Effects on the Provision of Public Services

To the extent that TDRs are effective, in conjunction with zoning, in
limiting development to certain areas and clustering it in higher
density groupings, the costs of certain public services may be reduced.
Naturally, zoning ordinances would have to be designed with this end in
mind.

In cases where development costs are actually increased with the
introduction of TDRs, the efficient provision of public services may be
encumbered rather than facilitated if the increased development costs
stimulate development to sprawl out into areas beyond the preservation zone. This underscores the need for having a relatively large
preservation zone—which, as the market analysis has shown, may be
difficult to sustain.

Distribution in a TDR System

The preceding analysis has indicated a variety of aspects of market
performance that will determine the distribution of material benefits
and costs among the groups affected by the institution of a TDR
system. Specifically, the elasticity of demand for housing and other
buildings and the elasticity of supply of urban land can be expected to
play key roles in the distribution of impacts. Whether or not initial
down-zoning is required to create adequate TDR demand will also be
important. These factors will also influence whether or not a true
"windfall-for-wipeout" type of transfer is brought about.

If housing demand is elastic and it is not necessary to down-zone to
create a demand for development-rights transfer, the introduction of
TDRs will actually cause an expansion in housing construction as
cheap TDRs are substituted for land. If the supply of urban land is
relatively elastic under these circumstances, a large number of TDRs
may be purchased before demand weakens. If the supply of land is

inelastic, however, and land prices drop quickly, the demand for TDRs can also be expected to drop off rather quickly. In either case, transfers to TDR holders (sellers) will come from a combination of reduced land sales and prices. Urban land suppliers will pay. But note that what is transferred from urban landowners in this case may not be a current windfall but may instead represent a reduction of land values that have appreciated in the past.[20] If this is the case, then these reductions would be no different from the "wipeouts" preservation-zone land-owners would have suffered if they had not been issued TDRs.

If initial down-zoning is required to create TDR demand, then developers would be forced either to use more land or to purchase TDRs. With elastic demand for housing, cost increases cannot be passed onto the homebuyer. Developers would be forced out of business, and land prices would consequently be depressed until equilibrium was reestablished. If the supply of urban land tends to be inelastic, then land prices will drop rather quickly and the development industry will be affected less severely than it would if the supply of land were more elastic on the downward side.

When the demand for housing and other types of developed buildings is not elastic, prices of these items may be either increased or decreased with the introduction of TDRs. Once again, the outcome depends upon whether or not initial down-zoning is required. If no down-zoning is required, the substitution of TDRs for land will lead simultaneously to expanded rates of development and reduced land prices. Landowners will sell less land at lower prices. Not only will some of the land cost savings be transferred to TDR sellers, but homebuyers will also benefit from reduced prices and developers will experience expanded production and sales opportunities.

If initial down-zoning is necessary and demand is not elastic, however, housing development costs will increase and this increase will be only partially offset by the purchase of TDRs to substitute for land. In this case, homebuyers and renters will pay higher prices and ultimately pay part of the cost of TDRs.

Equity in TDR Systems

The preceding analysis illustrates the difficulty of generalizing about the distributive effects of TDRs. In this sense, the equity of TDRs

---

20. Since no down-zoning was required to create TDR demand, no land price increases will result from the initiation of TDRs per se. If the introduction of TDRs is accompanied by new or changed zoning ordinances that reduce the supply of developable land, however, then current unearned increments in land values (windfalls) will arise, and these would be reduced or removed by the drop in land prices and sales that accompanies the introduction of TDRs.

is also indeterminate, although, as shown in Chapter 3, there are many ways of looking at equity, and TDR is a system designed with certain concepts of equity in mind.

Zoning ranks relatively high in terms of procedural equity. It typically allows ample citizen participation in plan formulation, and variance procedures provide recourse to those unfairly treated or inadequately represented in plan formulation. While some interest groups may be more effectively organized to participate than others, zoning has nevertheless been designed with a view to procedural equity or fairness. Once zoning decisions have been made, however, and windfalls or wipeouts result, there is no means for those who suffer material losses to be compensated. In other words, zoning is ill-equipped to deal with the allocative aspects of land use control. In this sense it is an inequitable system.

Zoning by Eminent Domain, discussed in Chapter 6 and Transferable Development Rights are both systems designed to make up for the allocative deficiencies of traditional zoning—both have a potential for addressing allocative aspects of equity with which zoning per se is not equipped to deal. Yet both ZED and TDR are limited treatments of zoning's allocative impacts. TDRs deal only with reallocating the specific, direct effects of zoning that fall on certain landowners. While ZED could in principle deal with indirect impacts, the discussion in Chapter 6 indicates that this would probably be difficult in practice. In any case, both systems deal only with reallocating impacts on landowners and deal with equity only in this way. They do not attempt to get at the more general allocative impacts of zoning between groups—between renters and new home buyers on the one hand and landowners on the other. In attempting to provide equity among landowners, ZED and TDRs may actually force up the price of new housing for example, causing a deterioration in the wealth–income position of renters and new home buyers in order to preserve the status quo among landowners.

Political Acceptability

As indicated in Chapter 4 and in an earlier paper by Godwin and Shepard (1975), land use policy has traditionally been dominated by developers and allied interest groups like savings and loan institutions, on the one hand, and by neighborhood groups organized on ad hoc bases to protest land use decisions. "Environmentalists" have emerged as a third group in recent years and have a special interest in public goods such as the preservation of critical natural areas which the TDR system may help to provide.

The present analysis of TDRs has singled out the interests of landowners. Many landowners may be developers. In fact, developers can be expected to own lands in both the development and preservation zones created by TDRs. This fact may serve to divide the interests of the development group. Landowners in preservation zones who have not yet sold their land to speculator–developers may be represented by farm interest groups which have already begun to take an interest in land use planning. Farm groups may well favor the TDR approach since it offers to help keep lands in agriculture and open space while paying the landowners for doing so.

The analysis has shown that renters and potential new home buyers have a vital stake in the TDR system, should it be adopted. As indicated earlier by Godwin and Shepard, however, members of this group are not usually organized to participate actively in land use planning. The emergence of renters' unions as an element to be contended with in some urban areas might provide a focus for these interests, although renters' groups have more frequently organized to act on core area housing problems. In other cases, mostly in major metropolitan centers, the poor have organized to exert themselves in housing policy. As renters and potential first-home buyers, the poor would be vitally affected in instances where the introduction of TDRs causes the cost of housing to increase and limits growth and new construction.

The TDR system is at a political disadvantage because it is not an incremental policy. It would represent a significant modification of the land use planning process and as the preceding analysis shows, its impacts are uncertain and depend heavily on how the market is structured. Even though many of the uncertainties—the method of initial rights distribution and the extent of the area to be covered—would have to be worked out and eliminated in advance of initiation, there are so many variable elements and unknown factors in the system that market performance is unpredictable. For example, we demonstrated that what is intended to be a "windfall-for-wipeout" compensation system could sometimes turn out to be a "wipeout-for-wipeout" system, with urban landowners suffering real drops in land values.

It is likely that some ongoing regulation of the TDR market would be required to secure an effective outcome from TDRs. Field and Conrad (1975, pp. 338–39) concluded that an open market would probably not be feasible and that the regulatory agency would have to act as an intermediary between buyer and seller to insure acceptable market performance. A centralized TDR brokerage agency to regulate an open market may make the plan more acceptable to some interest groups, particularly those well enough organized to influence and perhaps "capture" the agency.

In summary, TDRs do represent a new and different approach to land use planning. They may appeal greatly to environmentalists and, perhaps, to farm-interest groups, while dividing the interests of developers. While renters and new-home buyers would have much at stake should TDRs be used, they are not usually represented by organized interest groups. These considerations indicate that there might be some realistic political hope for the future of TDRs, but the great uncertainties associated with the system, together with the fact that it represents a radical departure from current zoning systems, serve to diminish this hope.

In final analysis, the political viability of the TDR approach will depend upon the particular situation in which it is attempted. At the start of the chapter, several TDR proposals were cited which have not been implemented. Only three limited applications have been made to date, one in a small town in Vermont, the other two with historical landmark preservation in New York City and in Washington D.C. It would be difficult to justify larger-scale applications until more information can be gained from these and other modest sized experiments.

✳ *Chapter 8*

Conclusions

> The comprehensive program whose many components are given equal
> emphasis and are pronounced to be interrelated in effect covers up the
> ignorance of the experts about the real cure of the malady they have been
> summoned to examine; if they knew, they would be proposing a far more
> sharply focused program (Hirschman 1967, p. 23).

The analyses of the preceding chapters may leave the reader
somewhat discouraged. We have shown that private land
use conflicts can occur and that society in general may have
to accommodate to a set of suboptimal efficiency and distribution outcomes. Public action may offer improvement in both. Yet zoning, the
most commonly employed tool of public intervention in the land market, leaves much to be desired on efficiency grounds. Zoning does not
provide a good mechanism for balancing the social benefits of land use
changes with the social costs.

Whether zoning causes a certain tract of land to be overdeveloped or
underdeveloped, considering all benefits and costs, depends upon the
actions of the participants in the zoning process and upon the rules
under which they operate. In the long run these decision rules evolve
from the political process and reflect the wishes of those groups who are
sufficiently enough affected to organize and participate in rule making.
As a result, zoning has been captured by important interest groups,
leaving the concerns of others unconsidered and raising serious equity
questions.

The groups most likely to be disadvantaged by expanding land use
planning and control are new-home buyers and renters. They have not
been well represented in land use control, and we could find little
reason to expect a dramatic change in their future participation. Most
public goods desired from land use control will unavoidably reduce the
supply of land for housing development. Unless increasing density
levels are allowed within existing residential areas, an action surely to
be fought by many current homeowners, the supply of certain types of

housing, most likely that within the means of low-income groups, may be significantly reduced.

While Zoning by Eminent Domain (ZED) and Transferable Development Rights (TDRs) address some of the problems of zoning, both systems work basically within the zoning framework. They can make zoning more effective, mainly by reducing the incentives that have traditionally caused comprehensive land use plans to be changed. But they can not accomplish efficiency objectives, which are simply out of zoning's reach. While ZED and TDRs can be viewed as extensions of zoning, their implementation would require significant changes in our system of land use planning. Because there is so little experience with them and because of the extent to which each situation may dramatically change their effects, their uncertainty of outcomes suggests that they will be politically unacceptable.

Perhaps we expect too much from land use planning, and as a result our standards for evaluating it may be too high. First, we may have been led to these high expectations because of the emphasis on "comprehensiveness" in so many planning circles. The ambitious scope of this type of planning may be a mistake. Comprehensiveness has at least two attributes.

The first relates to the spatial inclusiveness. Many advocate that all land be included in public planning efforts, but spatial inclusiveness per se provides no rationale for public concern. However, this error may be relatively small. The areas where the planning effort may be questioned are strictly rural, and here, even "comprehensive" planning may not be terribly costly. Furthermore, some of the costs may be offset by the long-run educational benefits of having a larger segment of the population involved.

The second attribute of comprehensiveness is the range of social concerns the planning process is to take into account. A review of state and local land use planning documents reveals a wide array of goals, including urban growth control, preservation of community life styles, energy conservation, and provision of adequate economic and employment opportunities (Fitch and Stoevener, in press). Although the quotation from Hirschman at the beginning of this chapter was directed at development planning, there may also be a need for more sharply focused programs in land use control. Some of the goals to be addressed by it are only indirectly related to land use allocation. A more specific delineation of goals directly related to land use conflicts is needed.

This is not to disregard the fact that land use planning is related to many other social goals, but land use planning is not likely to be the most effective means of achieving these objectives. Nor should it be assumed that causality in these interrelationships runs necessarily in only one direction. Programs specifically designed to accomplish these other objectives may have important impacts on land use as well. For example, there are frequent references to the interrelationships between land use and energy consumption. Yet land use planning is an unlikely candidate for dealing successfully with energy conservation goals. While certain energy savings can result from higher density and more contiguous residential developments, land use planning is an indirect and uncertain approach to gasoline conservation.

A gasoline conservation program would have to be broader based than one that reached only consumers who move into new residences, since only a portion of their gasoline consumption is determined in a significant way by the place where they live—commuting to work, shopping, medical facilities, etc. Another portion of automobile use is more discretionary, determined largely by the role of the automobile in personal or family life styles. A necessary condition for an effective gasoline conservation program is that the scarcity value of gasoline be taken into account by *all users* for *all purposes.* Having this value reflected in the price of gasoline is an effective way to transmit this information to consumers. One also expects that consumers, in turn, would consider commuting costs in their residential location decisions, so that the pursuit of another social objective, energy conservation, would have an impact on land use.

Our analysis may have been based on unrealistic expectations for a second reason—the very demanding formal evaluation criteria employed in this study. Perhaps one should not expect an endeavor that seeks to regulate the complex system of individual decisions relating to land use to meet high standards of efficiency or to rate highly on distributional grounds. ZED and TDRs would not make the system less complex. But note that these deficiencies were often identified as the results of unfulfilled informational and administrative requirements that would have to be met for the system to achieve the broad efficiency or distributional objectives specified for this study; objectives also typically specified by advocates of these techniques. If one were willing to settle for less, these requirements would decrease correspondingly.

The exercise performed in this study of closely analyzing each technique with respect to a set of efficiency considerations and distributive effects may prove helpful to those interested in improving land use control. By exposing areas in which each technique may be deficient, public-policy decision-makers and the general public interested in land use control may adjust unrealistic expectations of what each technique may do. They may also realize the possibility of unanticipated negative effects. Understanding the complexity of the land use allocation process and the potential for harm as well as benefit may lead to more modest and specifically directed efforts at resolving land use conflicts.

Rather than one control technique to treat all of the efficiency criteria discussed in Chapter 2, a number of specific techniques to deal with specific land use objectives may prove more satisfactory from both efficiency and equity perspectives. Some examples may help illustrate this point.

The analysis of zoning indicated that its attempts to reduce harmful external effects may suffer because these effects are not directly identified and controlled. In this regard, the application of performance standards deserves more serious investigation. Standards based on noise, fire danger, waste production, esthetics, and psychological effects would directly reflect the external effects of concern (Horack 1952, Stockham 1974). In addition, the requirement of establishing allowable quantitative limits for the regulated effects should provide less opportunity for employing indirect measures, e.g. minimum lot sizes, for racial or class exclusionary purposes.

ZED and TDRs represent a potential improvement over zoning for providing public goods, e.g., open space, but while they partially or fully compensate restricted landowners, they assess only some of the beneficiaries. Given the varying nature of the public goods of interest, increased reliance on specific public investment actions such as conservation easements, land banking, and eminent domain–special assessment proceedings may offer a better mechanism for insuring an adequate supply of these goods while not imposing all of the costs on restricted landowners. With these various forms of public investment, care has to be taken to ensure that the taxation revenue sources used to finance public good provision correspond to the primary beneficiaries of the good, otherwise those not required to pay will continue to demand an "oversupply."

Alternative public service pricing policies that incorporate the variation in provision costs attributable to development density and contiguity and capital replacement or expansion needs might aid the more efficient provision of public services.[1] This might be accomplished without the disregard for residential location preferences that is so characteristic of direct regulation.

Since these approaches to land use objectives can be viewed as incremental changes, their political acceptability may be greater, because their outcomes are more predictable than those of either ZED or TDRs. Of course, even the political acceptability of marginal changes

1. For case study examples of determining sewer charges, see Vars (1976).

will depend on the extent to which perceived social benefits significantly outweigh social costs and upon the relative political influence of those expecting to gain or lose. However, in general, specific proposals for incremental changes are politically more realistic than those which depart drastically from current practice.

There should be a final caveat about political acceptability: it is as difficult to predict as many other important social variables. There are many examples of public policy changes that would have been reckoned politically unfeasible at an earlier time. In no case should a proposal's low score on the political acceptability scale discourage us from experimenting with it. In the process we may learn much about the technique, gain insights into the operation of related systems of land use planning, and even discover a new system which, while comprehensive, is also efficient, equitable, and politically acceptable.

Bibliography

Alonso, William. *Location and Land Use, Toward General Theory of Land Rent.* Cambridge: Harvard University Press, 1964.

Anderson, William. "Zoning in Minnesota: Eminent Domain vs. Police Power." *National Municipal Review* 16, 1927, p. 624.

Babcock, Richard F. *The Zoning Game: Municipal Practices and Policies.* Madison: The University of Wisconsin Press, 1966.

Babcock, Richard F. and Fred P. Bosselman. *Exclusionary Zoning: Land Use Regulation and Housing in the 1970's.* New York: Praeger, 1973.

Bachrach, Peter and Morton S. Baratz. *Power and Poverty.* New York: Oxford University Press, 1970.

Barlowe, Raleigh. *Land Resource Economics: The Economics of Real Property.* Englewood Cliffs, N.J.: Prentice-Hall, 1972.

Barron, James C. and F. Thompson, *Impacts of Open Space Taxation in Washington,* Bulletin 772, Washington Agricultural Experiment Station, Pullman, March 1973.

Barrows, Richard L. and Bruce A. Prenguber. "Transfer of Development Rights: Analysis of a New Land Use Policy Tool." *American Journal of Agricultural Economics* 57, November 1975, pp. 549–557.

Bergman, Edward M. *Eliminating Exclusionary Zoning: Reconciling Workplace and Residence in Suburban Areas.* Cambridge, Mass: Ballinger, 1974.

Bergstrom, T.C. and Robert Goodman. "Private Demand for Public Goods." *American Economic Review* 63, June 1973, pp. 280–296.

Black, Duncan. *The Theory of Committees and Elections.* Cambridge: At the University Press, 1968.

Bosselman, Fred P., David Callies, and John Banta. *The Taking Issue.* Washington: Council on Environmental Quality, 1973.

Breton, Albert B. *The Economic Theory of Representative Government.* Chicago: Aldine, 1974.

167

Brewster, J.M. "The Impact of Technical Advance and Migration on Agricultural Society and Policy." *Journal of Farm Economics* 41, 1959, pp. 1169–1184.

Brigham, Eugene F. "The Determinants of Land Values." *Land Economics* 41, November 1965, pp. 325–334.

Buchanan, James M. and W.C. Stubblebine. "Externality." *Economica* 29, November 1962, pp. 371–384.

Buchanan, James and Gordon Tullock. *The Calculus of Consent.* Ann Arbor: University of Michigan Press, 1962.

Bureau of Governmental Research and Service. *Compensatory Land Use Regulations: Proposals, Issues, and Questions.* Planning Bulletin No. 7. University of Oregon, Eugene, 1975.

Campbell, Angus, Philip E. Converse, Warren E. Miller, and Donald E. Stokes. *The American Voter.* New York: John Wiley and Sons, 1960.

Carter, Harold O. et al. "Future Land Requirements to Produce Food for an Expanding World Population," in *Perspectives on Prime Lands.* Washington: U.S. Dept. of Agriculture, July 1975.

Castle, Emery N. and R. Bruce Rettig. "Land Use Conflicts and Their Resolution." *Journal of Soil and Water Conservation,* September–October 1972, pp. 207–210.

Chavooshian, B. Budd, George H. Nieswand, and Thomas Norman. "Growth Management Program . . . a Proposed New Approach to Local Planning and Zoning." Leaflet No. 503, Cooperative Extension Service, Rutgers University, New Brunswick, N.J., June 1974.

Clark, Richard T. "Predicted Economic Effects of Environmental Quality Control Policies on Linear Firm Models, and An Application to an Irrigated Farm Model." Unpublished Ph.D. dissertation, Oregon State University, Corvallis, 1972.

Clark, Richard T. "Transferable Development Rights: Some Problems in Evaluation." Paper presented at Land Use Planning Workshop, Battelle Seattle Research Center, Seattle, December 1974.

Clawson, Marion. "Economic and Social Conflicts in Land Use Planning." *Natural Resources Journal* 15, July 1975, pp. 473–490.

Clawson, Marion. *Suburban Land Conversion in the United States: An Economic and Governmental Process.* Baltimore: Johns Hopkins Press, 1971.

Coke, James G. and Charles S. Liebman. "Political Values and Population Density Control." *Land Economics* 37, 1961, pp. 347–361.

Committee on Environment and Land Use, "Senate Bill 849", Oregon Legislative Assembly, 1973 Regular Session, Salem, Oregon.

Costonis, John J. "Development Rights Transfer: An Exploratory Essay." *Yale Law Journal* 83, November 1973, pp. 75–128.

Costonis, John J. " 'Fair' Compensation and the Accommodation Power: Antidotes for the Taking Impasse in Land Use Controversies." *Columbia Law Review* 75, October 1975, pp. 1021–1082.

Costonis, John J. "The Chicago Plan: Incentive Zoning and the Preservation of Urban Landmarks." *Harvard Law Review,* 1972, pp. 574–631.

Costonis, John J. and Robert S. DeVoy. "The Puerto Rican Plan: Environmental Protection Through Development Rights Transfer," in *Transfer of Development Rights* (Jerome G. Rose, editor). New Brunswick: Center for Urban Policy Research (Rutgers) and the State University of New Jersey, 1975, pp. 200–209.

Crecine, John P., Otto A. Davis, and John E. Jackson. "Urban Property Markets: Some Empirical Results and Their Implications for Municipal Zoning." *Journal of Law and Economics* 10, October 1967, pp. 79–100.

Dahl, Robert. *Who Governs?* New Haven: Yale University Press, 1961.

Daly, Herman E. "Toward a Stationary-State Economy," in *Patient Earth* (John Harte and Robert H. Socolow, editors). New York: Holt, Rinehart and Winston, 1971, pp. 226–244.

Davis, Otto A. "Economic Elements in Municipal Zoning Decision." *Land Economics* 39, November 1963, pp. 375–386.

Day, L.B. Speech by L.B. Day, Director, Oregon Land Conservation and Development Commission, given at Oregon State University, Corvallis, February 10, 1976.

Delafons, John. *Land-Use Controls in the United States.* Cambridge: The MIT Press, Joint Center for Urban Studies, 1969.

Doubleday, D. Jay, R. Kenneth Godwin, and Kathleen Orange. *Citizen Participation in Planning for Coastal Zone Management.* Corvallis: Oregon State University, Sea Grant Publishing, 1976.

Downing, Paul B. "User Charges and the Development of Urban Land." *National Tax Journal* 26, December 1973, pp. 631–637.

Easton, David and Jack Dennis. *Children in the Political System: Origins of Political Legitmacy.* New York: McGraw-Hill, 1969.

Edelman, Murray. *Politics as Symbolic Action: Mass Arousal and Quiescence.* Chicago: Markham, 1971.

Edelman, Murray. *The Symbolic Uses of Politics.* Urbana: The University of Illinois Press, 1967.

Erlandson, Mark J. "The Distribution of Home, Business, and Speculative Real Estate Ownership among Income Classes." Unpublished Master's thesis, Oregon State University, Corvallis, 1976.

Etzioni, Amitai. *The Active Society: A Theory of Societal and Political Processes.* New York: The Free Press, 1968.

Field, Barry C. and Jon M. Conrad. "Economic Issues in Programs of Transferable Development Rights." *Land Economics* 51, November 1975, pp. 331–340.

Fitch, James B. and H.H. Stoevener, "Some Economic Perspectives of Land Use Planning," in *Economic Issues in Land Use Planning* (D.M. Sorensen and H.H. Stoevener, eds.) Western Rural Development Center, Oregon State University, Corvallis (in print).

Friedrich, Carl J. *Man and His Government.* New York: McGraw-Hill, 1963.

Galanter, Marc. "Why the 'Haves' Come Out Ahead: Speculations on the Limits of Legal Change." *Law & Society Review* 9, Fall 1974, pp. 95–151.

Gibbs, Christopher J.N. "An Economic Study of Sewage Transmission and

Land Use: An Empirical Application." Unpublished Ph.D. dissertation, Oregon State University, Corvallis, June 1973.

Godwin, R. Kenneth and W. Bruce Shepard. "Political Processes and Public Expenditures: A Re-Examination Based on Theories of Representative Government." *American Political Science Review* 70, December 1976.

Godwin, R. Kenneth and W. Bruce Shepard. "State Land Use Politics: Winners and Losers." *The Environmental Law Review* 5, Spring, 1975, pp. 703-726.

Goodman, William J. "Descriptive Information on Transfer of Development Rights, Accompanying Proposed Legislation" in *Transfer of Development Rights* (Jerome G. Rose, editor). New Brunswick: Center for Urban Policy Research (Rutgers) and the State University of New Jersey, 1975, pp. 210-220.

Gustafson, Gregory C. and L.T. Wallace, "Differential Assessment as Land Use Policy: The California Case," *Journal of the American Institute of Planners*, Vol. 41, Number 6, November 1975.

Hagman, Donald G. "Windfalls for Wipeouts," in *The Good Earth of America: Planning Our Land Use* (C. Lowell Harris, editor). Englewood Cliffs, N.J.: Prentice-Hall, 1974, pp. 109-133.

Hagman, Donald G. "Windfalls for Wipeouts: A Preliminary Report," in *Management and Control of Growth*. (Randall W. Scott, editor). Washington: The Urban Land Institute, 1975, pp. 275-289.

Hagman, Donald G. "Zoning by Special Assessment Financed Eminent Domain." *University of Florida Law Review* 28, in press, and in *Windfalls for Wipeouts* (D. Hagman and D. Misczynski, editors), American Society of Planning Officials, forthcoming.

Hamilton, Bruce. "Property Taxes and the Tiebout Hypothesis: Some Empirical Evidence," in *Fiscal Zoning and Land Use Controls* (Edwin Mills and Wallace Oates, editors). Lexington, Mass.: D.C. Heath, Lexington Books, 1975.

Hansen, David E. and S.I. Schwartz. "Landowner Behavior at the Rural-Urban Fringe in Response to Preferential Property Taxation." *Land Economics* 51, November 1975, pp. 341-354.

Harris, R.N.S., G.S. Tolley, and C. Harrell. "The Residential Site Choice." *Review of Economics and Statistics* 50, May 1968, pp. 241-247.

Horack, Frank E., Jr. "Performance Standards in Residential Zoning." *Planning*, 1952, pp. 153-161, reprinted in *Urban Land Use Policy: The Central City* (Richard B. Andrews, editor). New York: The Free Press, 1972, pp. 74-80.

Institute for Environmental Studies. *The Plan and Program for the Brandywine*. Philadelphia: University of Pennsylvania, 1968.

Internal Revenue Service. *Statistics of Income 1962 and 1972*. Washington: Government Printing Office.

Ishee, Sidney. "'Transferable Development Rights' as a Means of Influencing Land Use Patterns." Paper presented at Land-Use Planning Workshop, Batelle Seattle Research Center, Seattle, December 1974.

Jaros, Dean. *Socialization to Politics*. New York: Praeger, 1973.

Kain, John F. and John M. Quigley. *Housing Markets and Racial Discrimi-*

nation: A Microeconomic Analysis. New York: National Bureau of Economic Research, 1975.

Katora, G., L. Mardell, and J. Schmiedeskamp. *Survey of Consumer Finances (1962, 1970).* Ann Arbor, Mich.: Survey Research Center, 1963, 1971.

King, A. and Peter Mieszkowski. "Racial Discrimination, Segregation, and the Price of Housing." *Journal of Political Economy* 81, May/June 1973, pp. 590-606.

Knetsch, Jack L. "Land Values and Parks in Urban Fringe Areas." *Journal of Farm Economics* 44, December 1962, pp. 1718-1729.

Krutilla, John V. "Is Public Intervention in Water Resources Development Conducive to Economic Efficiency?" *National Resources Journal* 6, January 1966, pp. 60-75.

Lindblom, Charles E. *The Intelligence of Democracy.* New York: The Free Press, 1965.

Linowes, R. Robert and Don T. Allensworth. *The Politics of Land Use: Planning, Zoning, and the Private Developer.* New York: Praeger, 1973.

Lipset, Seymour Martin. *Political Man: The Social Bases of Politics.* New York: Doubleday, 1960.

Louis Harris and Associates. *The Public's View of Environmental Problems in the State of Oregon.* Portland: Louis Harris and Associates, 1970.

Lowenberg, Paul, assisted by Dean Misczynski, Davis Thompson, and Donald Hagman. *Windfalls for Wipeouts: An Annotated Bibliography of Betterment Recapture and Worsenment Avoidance Techniques in the United States, Australia, Canada, England, and New Zealand.* Monticello, Ill.: Council of Planning Librarians, Exchange Bibliography Nos. 618, 619, and 620: 1974.

Lowi, Theodore J. "American Business, Public Policy, Case Studies, and Political Theory." *World Politics* 16, July 1964, pp. 677-715.

Lowi, Theodore J. *The End of Liberalism: Ideology, Policy and the Crisis of Authority.* New York: W.W. Norton, 1969.

Maisel, Sherman J. "Background Information on Costs of Land for Single Family Housing," in *Appendix to the Report on Housing in California.* Governor's Advisory Commission on Housing Problems, April 1963, pp. 221-282.

Marcus, Norman and Marilyn W. Groves (editors). *The New Zoning: Legal, Administrative and Economic Concepts and Techniques.* New York: Praeger, 1970.

Massachusetts State Department of Commerce and Massachusetts Institute of Technology, Urban and Regional Studies Section. *The Effects of Large Lot Size on Residential Development.* Washington: Urban Land Institute, 1958.

McMillan, Melville. "Land-Use Control for the Preservation of Open Space on the Rural-Urban Fringe: An Alternative Policy." *Working Paper No. 7.* Madison: Center for Resource Policy Studies, University of Wisconsin, December 1973.

Merrifield, Lewis B., III. "The General Welfare, Welfare Economics, and Zoning Variances." *Southern California Law Review* 38, Summer 1965, pp. 548-593, reprinted in *Urban Land Use Policy: The Central City* (Richard B. Andrews, editor). New York: The Free Press, 1972, pp. 24-40.

Milbrath, Lester. *Political Participation*. Chicago: Rand McNally, 1965.

Mill, John Stuart. *Considerations on Representative Government*, edited with an introduction by Currin V. Shields. New York: Bobbs-Merrill, 1958.

Mills, Edwin S. "A Survey of Economic Issues Related to Urban Land Use Controls." Unpublished paper, Princeton University, 1976.

Mitchell, Joyce M. and William C. Mitchell. *Political Analysis and Public Policy: An Introduction to Political Science*. Chicago: Rand McNally, 1969.

Moore, Audrey. "Transferable Development Rights: An Idea Whose Time Has Come," in *Transfer of Development Rights* (Jerome G. Rose, editor) New Brunswick: Center for Urban Policy Research (Rutgers) and the State University of New Jersey, 1975, pp. 221–232.

Muller, Thomas. "Implicit Grants to Property Owners at the Local Level: A Case Study," in *Redistribution to the Rich and the Poor: The Grants Economics of Income Distribution* (Kenneth Boulding and Martin Pfaff, editors). Belmont, Calif.: Wadsworth, 1972.

Muth, Richard F. "The Derived Demand for Urban Residential Land." *Urban Studies* 8, October 1971, pp. 243–254.

Olson, Mancur, Jr. *The Logic of Collective Action: Public Goods and the Theory of Groups*. New York: Schocken, 1965.

Polsby, Nelson. *Community Power and Political Theory*. New Haven: Yale University Press, 1963.

Projector, D. and G. Weiss. *Survey of Financial Characteristics of Consumers*. Washington: Board of Governors of the Federal Reserve System, 1966.

Prothro, James W. and Charles M. Grigg. "Fundamental Principles of Democracy: Bases for Agreement and Disagreement." *Journal of Politics* 22, 1960, pp. 276–294.

Raleigh, James C. "What Price Zoning?" *Appraisal Journal* 32, 1964, p. 602.

Randall, Alan. "Market Solutions to Externality Problems: Theory and Practice." *American Journal of Agricultural Economics* 54, May 1972, pp. 175–183.

Real Estate Research Corporation. *The Costs of Sprawl: Detailed Cost Analysis: Environmental and Economic Costs of Alternative Residential Development Patterns at the Urban Fringe*. Washington: Government Printing Office, April 1974.

Reuter, Frederick H. "Externalities in Urban Property Markets: An Empirical Test of the Zoning Ordinance of Pittsburgh." *Journal of Law and Economics* 16, October 1973, pp. 313–350.

Richards, David. "Development Rights Transfer in New York City." *Yale Law Journal* 82, December 1972, pp. 338–372.

Ricker, William H. and Peter C. Ordeshook. "A Theory of the Calculus of Voting." *American Political Science Review* 62, March 1968, pp. 25–42.

Rose, Jerome G. (editor). *Transfer of Development Rights*. New Brunswick: Center for Urban Policy Research (Rutgers) and The State University of New Jersey, 1975.

Rose, Louis A. *Taxation of Land Value Increments Attributable to Rezoning*. Honolulu: Economic Research Center, University of Hawaii, 1971.

Ruttan, V.W. "Technology and the Environment." *American Journal of Agricultural Economics* 53, December 1971, pp. 707–717.

Sagalyn, Lynne and George Sternlieb. *Zoning and Housing Costs: The Impact of Land Use Controls on Housing Price.* New Brunswick, N.J.: Center for Urban Policy Research, Rutgers University, 1973.

Schefter, John E. "The Demand for and Supply of the Characteristics of a New Residence and the Residential Location Decision." Unpublished Ph.D. dissertation, Oregon State University, Corvallis, 1976.

Schlaes, Jared B. "Who Pays for Transfer of Development Rights?" *Planning* July 1974, pp. 7–9, reprinted in *Transfer of Development Rights* (Jerome G. Rose, editor). New Brunswick: Center for Urban Policy Research (Rutgers), and the State University of New Jersey, 1975.

Schnidman, Frank. "Growth Management in Ramapo and Petaluma." Report 3, Washington: Land Use Planning Reports, August 1974.

Siegan, Bernard H. *Land Use Without Zoning.* Lexington, Mass.: D.C. Heath, Lexington Books, 1972.

Stockham, John. *Performance Standards: A Technique for Controlling Land Use.* Corvallis: Special Report 424, Oregon State University Extension Service, November 1974.

Stull, William J. "Community Environment, Zoning, and the Market Value of Single-Family Homes." *The Journal of Law and Economics* 18, October 1975, pp. 535–557.

Toll, Seymour I. *Zoned American.* New York: Grossman, 1969.

Tullock, Gordon. "A Simple Algebraic Logrolling Model." *American Economic Review* 60, June 1970, pp. 419–426.

Vars, Charles R., Jr. "A Connection Charge for the City of Corvallis." Unpublished paper, Department of Economics, Oregon State University, Corvallis, 1976.

Vars, Charles R., Jr. "A Revised Cost Analysis of Sewerage Treatment Facilities for the City of Tillamook and the 101 North Sanitary District." Unpublished paper, Department of Economics, Oregon State University, Corvallis, 1976.

Vars, Charles R., Jr. "Evaluation of Proposed Sewer Charges for Douglas County at Salmon Harbor." Unpublished paper, Department of Economics, Oregon State University, Corvallis, 1976.

Verba, Sidney and Norman Nie. *Participation in America: Political Democracy and Social Equality.* New York: Harper & Row, 1972.

Wengert, Norman and Thomas Graham. "Transferable Development Rights and Land Use Control." *Journal of Soil and Water Conservation* 29, November–December 1974, pp. 253–257.

Wieand, Kenneth F. "Air Pollution and Property Values: A Study of the St. Louis Area." *Journal of Regional Science* 13, 1973, p. 341.

Wilson, Leonard U. "Precedent- Setting Swap in Vermont." *American Institute of Architects Journal*, 1974, pp. 51–52, reprinted in *Transfer of Development Rights* (Jerome G. Rose, editor). New Brunswick: Center for Urban Policy Research (Rutgers), and the State University of New Jersey, 1975.

Wolff, Robert Paul. "Beyond Tolerance," in *A Critique of Pure Tolerance* (Robert P. Wolff, Barrington More, and Herbert Marcuse, editors). Boston: Beacon Press, 1965.

Yaden and Associates, Inc. *Issues in Oregon.* Portland: Yaden and Associates, 1974.

Yeates, M.H. "The Effect of Zoning on Land Values in American Cities: A Case Study," in *Essays in Geography for Austin Miller* (J.B. Whittow and P.D. Wood, editors) Reading, U.K.: University of Reading Press, 1965.

INDEX: *Land Use Control,* David E. Ervin et al.

About the Authors

David E. Ervin was a research associate with the Department of Agricultural and Resource Economics, Oregon State University while completing this work and is now Assistant Professor of Agricultural Economics at the University of Missouri (Columbia). His B.S., M.S. (Ohio State University: 1967, 1969) and Ph.D. degrees (Oregon State University, 1974) were all taken in the field of agricultural economics. He has worked on problems in income determination and his current research and teaching interests are in the field of natural resource economics, with specific focus on the role of land.

James B. Fitch is Assistant Professor of Agricultural and Resource Economics at Oregon State University. His B.S. degree (Stanford, 1961) was taken in Mathematics, while his M.S. (Purdue, 1969) and Ph.D. (Stanford, 1974) degrees were in agricultural and applied economics. Dr. Fitch's current research interests include both domestic and international resource development and agricultural development. His interest in urban fringe land development stems from earlier research on the impacts of population growth on local government finances. He has recently served as a consultant to two American Indian tribes on the development of agricultural land resources.

R. Kenneth Godwin is Associate Professor and Chairman of the Department of Political Science, Oregon State University. His major teaching and research interests are political behavior, public policy and political demography. He was formerly associated with the Battelle Human Affairs Research Centers and the Carolina Population Center. He received his Ph.D. from the University of North Carolina in 1971.

W. Bruce Shepard is Assistant Professor of Political Science at Oregon State University. He received his Ph.D. from the University of California (Riverside). He has worked on and written about migration, land use policy, political participation, population policy, political representation, and metropolitan political organization.

Herbert H. Stoevener is Professor of Agricultural and Resource Economics at Oregon State University. After he grew up in Germany he studied agriculture at Cornell University and obtained M.S. and Ph.D. degrees in Agricultural Economics from the University of Illinois. At Oregon State University he is teaching and doing research in the economics of natural resources management with special emphasis on environmental and land use issues.